RESTORING
MARGIN
TO
OVERLOADED
LIVES

RESTORING
MARGIN
TO
OVERLOADED
LIVES

A COMPANION WORKBOOK TO *MARGIN* AND *THE OVERLOAD SYNDROME*

RICHARD A. SWENSON, M.D. with Karen Lee-Thorp

NAVPRESS®

BRINGING TRUTH TO LIFE

OUR GUARANTEE TO YOU

We believe so strongly in the message of our books that we are making this quality guarantee to you. If for any reason you are disappointed with the content of this book, return the title page to us with your name and address and we will refund to you the list price of the book. To help us serve you better, please briefly describe why you were disappointed. Mail your refund request to: NavPress, P.O. Box 35002, Colorado Springs, CO 80935.

The Navigators is an international Christian organization. Our mission is to reach, disciple, and equip people to know Christ and to make Him known through successive generations. We envision multitudes of diverse people in the United States and every other nation who have a passionate love for Christ, live a lifestyle of sharing Christ's love, and multiply spiritual laborers among those without Christ.

NavPress is the publishing ministry of The Navigators. NavPress publications help believers learn biblical truth and apply what they learn to their lives and ministries. Our mission is to stimulate spiritual formation among our readers.

NAVPRESS, BRINGING TRUTH TO LIFE, and the NAVPRESS logo are registered trademarks of NavPress. Absence of ® in connection with marks of NavPress or other parties does not indicate an absence of registration of those marks.

ISBN 1-57683-184-1

Cover photo by Trevor Bonderud/Westlight
Creative Team: Tim Howard, Darla Hightower

Some of the anecdotal illustrations in this book are true to life and are included with the permission of the persons involved. All other illustrations are composites of real situations, and any resemblance to people living or dead is coincidental.

Sidebar excerpts that are not otherwise noted are taken from *Margin* or *The Overload Syndrome*.

Unless otherwise identified, all Scripture quotations in this publication are taken from the *HOLY BIBLE: NEW INTERNATIONAL VERSION* ® (NIV). Copyright © 1973, 1978, 1984 by International Bible Society. Used by permission of Zondervan Publishing House. All rights reserved. Other versions used include: the *New King James Version* (NKJV), copyright © 1979, 1980, 1982, 1990, Thomas Nelson Inc., Publishers.

Printed in the United States of America

2 3 4 5 6 7 8 9 10 11 12 13 14 15 16 / 09 08 07 06 05 04

Dedication

This workbook is dedicated to
all those wishing
to make space in their lives
for the things that matter most.

Acknowledgments

This workbook, a long time in coming, has grown out of readers of *Margin* and *The Overload Syndrome* requesting additional tools for application. To those who have thus stimulated this project with their interest I am indebted.

The bulk of my gratitude rightfully extends to Karen Lee-Thorp for her thoughtful workbook format. Her well-acknowledged expertise and experience are on display throughout this easy-to-use yet provocative volume. She employed both a thoughtful guidance and appropriate level of challenge as she shaped the workbook element. Many other people at NavPress have likewise been supportive and professional. As always, thanks.

I am also grateful to Christian Business Men's Committee, Ron Soderquist in his Pentagon work, Bill Peel at CMDS's Tournier Institute, and Dallas Christian Video, each of whom have previously produced margin study guides and worksheets.

My wife, Linda, once again addressed this manuscript with precision. Her tireless thoroughness never ceases to amaze me. I am continually grateful for her efforts, and the reader—if you only knew—would be as well.

Contents

Introduction

Almost everyone today has experienced stress. We know all too much about stress. But few of us have even heard of the solution to stress: margin.

What is margin? Margin is the space between your load and your limits. If you are chronically overloaded—if you don't have enough time, money, physical energy, or emotional energy to accomplish the tasks of a given week or month—then you are heading for system failure. Before you hit burnout (or even if you feel you're already there), it would be wise to address your overload and gain some margin in your life.

My books *Margin* and *The Overload Syndrome* explain in detail both the problem of overload and the solution of margin. This workbook is designed to help you assess and deal with the overload in your life in specific, practical ways. It will help you make changes on three fronts:

- *What you know*. You will need to understand some things: What is overload? What is margin? What is the role of progress in creating overload? Are humans designed to have limits? Some questions in this workbook will help you digest the concepts in *Margin* and *The Overload Syndrome.*
- *What you feel, believe, and want in your heart of hearts.* If you're going to make lasting changes in your life, you will need to look inside yourself to see the desires, beliefs, and feelings that motivate you. What do you really want in life? What do you believe it takes to get your deepest desires met? What makes you anxious? Some exercises in this workbook will help you examine these motivators. You will have a chance to consider whether what you thought you wanted in life is really what you want to live for. Also, you will get to think about where your beliefs come from: For example, if the media are telling you how

to get your deepest desires met, are they telling you the truth? Finally, you will address your fears—perhaps the fear of losing or failing in your job—and decide what you want to do about them.

- *What you do.* You will survey your life—from activities to expenses to information—and make realistic plans for the coming six months. What will your priorities be? What will you cut back on or give up? What steps can you take to guard your time, reduce your debt, build emotional reserves, and invest in the people and pursuits that really matter to you?

This workbook is divided into twelve sessions. Each of the first ten sessions should take you about an hour to complete, depending on the depth at which you reflect on the questions. Sessions 11 and 12 may each take as much as two hours, because in those sessions you will create a realistic action plan for the next six months. You may work at your own pace, and it's not necessary to finish a whole session in one sitting. However, there is a certain logic to each session that will bring you to a place of decision and prayer at the end of each one.

You can use the workbook on your own, with your spouse, or with a group of friends or coworkers. It's enormously helpful to have some support as you think through these issues, but if you prefer to work alone, you should have no trouble doing so. The questions and exercises are designed to be done privately, and then you may meet with a group to discuss them if you so choose. At the end of each session you will see instructions for groups.

For Groups

If you are meeting with a group, there are a few housekeeping details to take care of before you dive into session 1. First, unless you already know each other well, it's helpful to exchange some basic information. Second, it's wise to spell out your expectations and ground rules so that people know what they are committing themselves to.

Consider making your first meeting a meal—perhaps a potluck or bring-your-own-lunch—so that people have some time to get to know each other in a relaxed setting. The following is a possible outline for the agenda portion of this meeting. This agenda assumes that group members are seeing the workbook for the first time, that the purpose and schedule of the group have not already been set, and that you want to take care of all this housekeeping in the first meeting. In this way, you can get right into the meat of the workbook in your first meeting. Another option is to spread these tasks over several meetings.

1. Let the discussion leader—or someone familiar with the workbook—take five minutes or less to sketch for the group what the workbook contains.

2. Allow each person to take one minute to tell three things about himself or herself that have *nothing* to do with his or her work. These can be favorite nonwork activities, qualities in you that annoy your spouse, qualities in you that your friends enjoy, the number of times you have changed your address in the past five years—any nonwork information that will help people know you.

3. Imagine you're a car that runs on physical, emotional, and spiritual fuel. How full is your gas tank? Rank it from 0 (empty or just fumes) to 10 (full).

4. What motivates you to use a workbook on overload and margin? What do you hope to get out of this group? Allow each person a minute to answer these questions.

5. This workbook contains twelve sessions. Ideally, you will meet weekly for twelve weeks, and each meeting will take ninety minutes. Ideally, you will come to each meeting having read and written answers to the questions in the session you will discuss. However, if you need a workbook on margin, chances are that the ideal will not seem realistic to everyone. Take some time to come to consensus on these questions:

   ■ *How frequently will you meet?* (Weekly? Every other week? Less often?) If you meet less often than every other week, you may find yourselves losing continuity. It's hard to remember what someone said a month ago. But if you have to meet monthly, so be it.

- *How long will your meetings be?* If you have only fifty minutes over lunch, that will have to do. The discussion leader will need to select just a few questions from each session that seem most important to discuss. You could plan to discuss just a couple of standard questions: What seemed especially relevant in this session? What questions or challenges did it raise for you? What have you done this week/month to address your margin problem?

- *How much time can you give each week to doing the workbook exercises on your own?* Be honest about this. There's no reason why you can't take two meetings to cover a session. In particular, sessions 11 and 12 may require extra time.

- *To what extent can you make this group a priority?* For instance, if your travel schedule requires you to miss half the meetings, that will be a problem. Is it possible to schedule your travel around the meetings or the meetings around your travel? Also, does this group compete with your family commitments, or does your family see this group as potentially helping you make more time for them in the long run? A group like this won't work well if members have to miss more than a couple of meetings. Consider setting a ground rule that no one will miss more than two meetings. Is that realistic for you? If not, say so now.

6. Discuss leadership. It's a good idea to have one person responsible for coordinating details, such as notifying people if the location of a meeting needs to change. However, it's possible to rotate the responsibility for facilitating the discussions. The facilitator's job is to select which questions you will discuss at a given meeting, keep the discussion on track, and watch the clock.

7. Agree on a purpose statement for your group. This statement need not be as carefully crafted as a corporate mission statement, but it should be clear enough to let people know if their desires conflict sharply. Consider the difference

between these two statements:

- **Our group exists to discuss** the concepts of overload and margin so that we can better understand the pressures we face.
- **Our group exists to support** its members in decreasing overload in their lives.

The first statement above focuses on discussion of information. The second focuses on support for change. What are your group's goals?

8. The following are ground rules that many groups find helpful. Read the list, and discuss anything you would like to add or change.

   a. The reason our group exists is:
   b. Our specific group goals include:
   c. We meet _____ time(s) a month.
   d. We will meet on _____ (day of week), from _____ A.M./P.M. to _____ A.M./P.M.
   e. Our meetings will be at _____ (place[s]).
   f. We agree to maintain the following disciplines (choose one or more):

   □ *Attendance*: This group will be a priority for me. I will not miss more than two meetings. I will notify the leader if I will be late or absent.
   □ *Ownership*: I agree to share responsibility for the group and our goals.
   □ *Confidentiality*: I agree to keep here whatever is shared here.
   □ *Accountability*: I give permission to the other group members to hold me accountable for goals I set for myself.

9. Take five minutes to evaluate this group session. What went well? What would you like to improve for next time?

10. Pray. First, have someone read aloud the quotation from

Henri Nouwen on page 51 of this workbook. Then allow a minute of silence. Ask God to use these next few weeks and months to create some space in your lives in which God can act. Pray for space. Then allow some time in which group members can add their own prayers, either silently or aloud, for the concerns on their minds. Close with thanks for the opportunity to set out on this journey together.

Margin, Load, and Limits

Nobody who needs a workbook on margin is likely to feel he or she has the time to do it. If you're feeling overwhelmed at the thought of taking on this task, or guilty over what you're not doing right now, then you're probably right where you belong! Take thirty seconds right now to ask God to run the universe for the next hour so that you can invest in this workbook. And if you need to complete this first session fifteen minutes at a time, that's okay.

Your objectives in this session are:

- To understand the concepts of margin, overload, and limits
- To observe your immediate gut reaction to the idea that you might have limits
- To spend five minutes being still in the presence of God

What's margin? *Margin* is the amount available beyond that which is needed. It is something held in reserve for contingencies or unanticipated situations. It is the leeway between ourselves and our limits. The math is simple:

$$\text{Power - Load = Margin}$$

Power is made of up factors such as skills, time, emotional strength, physical strength, spiritual vitality, finances, social supports, and education.

Load combines internal factors (such as personal expectations and emotional disabilities) and external factors (such as work, relational problems and responsibilities, financial obligations, and civic involvement).[1]

When our power is greater than our load, we have margin. We have room to play within our budget, our bodies, our emotions, our schedules, and our relationships. We have some reserves with which to pay an unexpected bill, work a little extra during a crunch, or handle a family crisis.

No king is saved by the size of his army;
   no warrior escapes by his great strength. . . .
   But the eyes of the LORD are on those who fear him,
   on those whose hope is in his unfailing love,
   to deliver them from death
   and keep them alive in famine.
   (Psalm 33:16,18-19)

However, when our load is greater than our power, we have no margin. In fact, we're in *overload*. Endured long-term overload damages our physical, mental, spiritual, and relational health. When we are going flat out all the time, sooner or later something will snap.

It's easiest to think of financial margin. If we spend a little less than we earn each month, then we build up savings. When the refrigerator dies or we have hospital expenses, we can deplete our savings to pay for the emergency need. However, if we spend everything we earn each month, then unusual bills send us into debt. And if we regularly spend more than we earn, relying on credit cards and loans, then even a small crisis can send us into bankruptcy. Margin is spending less than we earn. Overload is habitually spending more.

1. Give one example from your life in which your load exceeds your capacity or power. (This is overload.)

2. Give one example from your life in which your power exceeds your load. (This is an area in which you have margin.)

SEVERAL years ago, a medical colleague became engaged. Having taught this delightful young physician, I was pleased to receive an invitation to the wedding.

They were to be married on an August afternoon at 3:00 P.M. As our home is a half-hour from the church, at 2:25 P.M. I loaded my family into the car and headed east. By my calculations, we would have thirty minutes to get to the church, five minutes to find a pew, and zero minutes to waste. The organ would start, the bride would begin down the aisle. . . .

As planned, we arrived in the church parking lot at precisely 2:55 P.M. Perfect timing. So far, so good. There was only one problem. The parking lot was empty. Completely empty. Not as in I'm early empty, but as in I've got the wrong church empty. There were seventy other churches in the city, and I had five minutes to find the right one. Normally a good problem solver, I came quickly to a plan. Linda, too, had a plan. The trouble was her plan and my plan were not the same plan. And, of course, neither would get us to the church on time.

I am not an irritable person, and Linda is even less so. But I was irritable right then. It was hot and I was starting to perspire. Linda and I exchanged conflicting suggestions for solving our dilemma and redeeming what was left of the wedding. Meanwhile our two delightful boys were in the back seat discussing how incompetent their parents were.

We finally found the church — but, of course, arrived twenty minutes late. Squeezing into a back pew, I had worked up an uncomfortable sweat. Somehow our anticipation of a delightful afternoon spent with friends celebrating the highlight of a life had not quite turned out as hoped.

We had left no margin for error. And we paid the price.

These notions of margin and overload assume that humans have *limits*. They assume that no matter how hard and long you work out, there is a limit to the amount of weight your biceps can lift. There is a minimum amount of sleep your body needs in a given week in order to maintain your mind and your immune system.

The human function curve (figure 1)[2] illustrates what happens when we push ourselves beyond our limits. Up to a point, our performance increases with increasing demand and increasing effort. But

In vain you rise early
   and stay up late,
   toiling for food to
eat—
   for he grants sleep to
those he loves.
   (Psalm 127:2)

beyond point A (our realistic limit), fatigue sets in, and performance begins to decline. Beyond point B (our absolute limit), we burn out. To live with margin would be to push ourselves regularly close to point A. Occasionally, for limited periods of time, we might push past point A in a crisis. We would avoid pushing ourselves to point B, and we would also be sure that periods of peak load would be followed by periods when we backed way off from point A in order to recover. That would be life at peak efficiency without self-destructiveness.

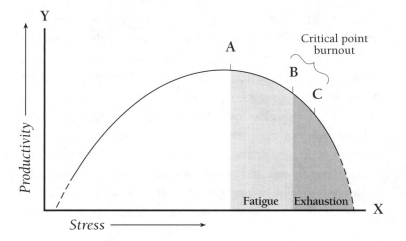

Figure 1: Human Function Curve

However, our world bombards us with messages that tell us not to believe in limits. Athletes are lauded for breaking records. No one likes to think that there is a limit to how fast any human will ever run a mile. We broke the four-minute mile—why not one minute? Thirty seconds? Five seconds?

The model of record-breaking suggests that we should become less and less limited with time. Traveling at the speed of sound was a limit years ago, but as technology improves, we can go faster and faster. As individuals, though, limits work in the opposite direction. We all become more physically limited as we age. Yet in our culture, we treat this fact as an outrage to be ignored out of existence. Why can't I get by on three hours of sleep a night as I did in medical school? Why can't I eat the way I did at twenty and not gain weight? If achievement and mastery are what give meaning to my life, then aging must inevitably terrify me.

If physical limits are hard for us to accept, emotional limits are even harder. They're invisible. Physically, most of us could carry a one-hundred-pound person on our back. But we could not carry ten. We would not even try. Our refusal would not be viewed as a statement against carrying people but as a statement about physical limits, about overload and pain. But translate this example to the emotional realm, and we get confused. We might be able to emotionally "carry" one person. But what about five? Ten? One hundred? Where should we draw the line? What boundaries should we establish? One of the most serious causes of Christians' emotional and spiritual struggles is "unclear boundaries."[3] The limits of emotional overload are hard to define, and helping people is one of the easiest places where emotional overload is manifested.

Mental limits are just as hard to define, but we know they exist. Cars can go faster and faster, but there is a limit to the speed at which a human can respond to turn the wheel or hit the brake. Information can so bombard us that we can remember nothing more. Air-traffic controllers are a prime example of too much mental stress too fast, and burnout on this job is routine.

3. Read the following list of limits. Check the box in the left column if you believe you are limited in this area. Check the box in the right column if you *live as though* you are limited in this area.

**I believe
I'm limited in this.** **I live like
I'm limited in this.**

☐ The distance I can run in an hour without collapsing ☐

☐ The number of stairs I can climb in an hour
without collapsing ☐

☐ The minimum amount of sleep I can get in a week
and still function effectively ☐

☐ The volume of groceries I can carry from my car to
my kitchen in one trip ☐

☐ The number of telephone calls I can give and receive
in one day ☐

☐ The length of time I can drive my car without
stopping to rest ☐

☐ The weight I can carry in a backpack for one mile ☐

☐ The minimum amount of food I can survive on
in a given year ☐

☐ The number of good decisions I can make in one day ☐

☐ The number of people I can support emotionally
during a given week ☐

continued

Our economy and our society are run by the driven. They climb to positions of power by force and then demand the same overcommitment from those under them.

I believe I'm limited in this.		I live like I'm limited in this.
☐	The number of clients/patients/customers I can serve in a given week	☐
☐	The number of angry people I can treat with kindness in a given week	☐
☐	The minimum amount of time alone I need in a given month	☐
☐	The minimum amount of time with loved ones I need in a given month	☐
☐	The number of new tasks I can learn to do in a given year	☐
☐	The amount of new information I can absorb in a given month	☐
☐	The minimum amount of time I need to get from my home to my workplace	☐

4. What did you learn about yourself from the above exercise?

5. In which of the following areas do you have trouble living within limits?

☐ Spending money
☐ Expecting performance from myself
☐ Expecting performance from others
☐ Getting enough sleep
☐ Getting enough rest
☐ Helping people
☐ Getting ahead in my career
☐ Getting another degree

☐ Partying
☐ Acquiring possessions
☐ Driving
☐ Eating
☐ Volunteering my time
☐ Other: _____
☐ Other: _____

6. What goes through your mind when someone suggests you have limits?

7. What messages do you get from your world that tell you not to believe you have limits? Consider, for example:

- TV commercials ("Just Do It")
- News about athletes who break records
- Demands from work supervisors
- Messages from church

God opposes the proud
but gives grace to the
humble.
   (James 4:6)

8. Some people argue that it's bad for society as a whole and for you as an individual to think of yourself as limited. Some say it's unChristian. What bad effects might result if you decided to live within limits?

Some people quote the apostle Paul—"I can do all things through Christ who strengthens me"[4]—to argue that believing in limits reflects lack of faith in an unlimited God. But when Paul said he could do all things, he meant all that God had given him to do. It's unlikely that Paul believed he could preach the gospel in every city in the Roman Empire before his death. He didn't even try. Jesus didn't minister to everyone in Palestine during His earthly life. Far from working twenty-hour ministry days, He took time off for rest and prayer, and He left towns with the people still clamoring for more healings.

I don't believe Christ chooses to strengthen me to do *all* things I might want to do. If I jumped off a cliff, I don't believe He would strengthen me to fly (see Luke 4:9-12). I don't believe He would strengthen me to live six months without eating, unless He had a specific reason for performing such a miracle. And I don't believe He enables people to live healthy lives chronically overloaded. God the Creator made us limited. Denying limits is not faith; it is pride.

I am not against load. Without load, life would be boring, and God has things for each of us to do. I'm against *over*load. I am not against being all that we can be. I'm against the arrogance that tries to be something we're not. I'm not even against stress (more on that in session 2). I'm against *distress*. God our Creator made limits and placed us within them to protect us and remind us that we are mortals and not gods. We exceed those limits at our peril.

9. God designed humans with limits—with needs such as food, water, and sleep. God even designed Adam to need a helper: Eve.[5] Adam wasn't built to run Eden on his own. Why do you suppose God designed us with limits? What spiritual benefits do our limits produce?

> The LORD God said, "It is not good for the man to be alone. I will make a helper suitable for him."
> (Genesis 2:18)

....

FROM 9:00 to 5:00 on weekdays, Candice is an office manager for a dentist. From 5:30 to 9:00 a.m., and then again from 5:00 to 11:00 p.m. plus weekends, Candice is a cook, housekeeper, chauffeur, psychologist, and referee. Candice has three children. She also has a husband, Dave, but since the kids were born, she and Dave have been growing more and more to be roommates and business partners, rather than best friends and sweethearts. Conversations go like this:

"Sean told me his throat was scratchy. Can you take his temperature?"
"Where's the thermometer?"
"Well, it should be in the bathroom cabinet, where it always is. . . ."

When the sun was setting, the people brought to Jesus all who had various kinds of sickness, and laying his hands on each one, he healed them. Moreover, demons came out of many people, shouting, "You are the Son of God!" But he rebuked them and would not allow them to speak, because they knew he was the Christ.

At daybreak Jesus went out to a solitary place. The people were looking for him and when they came to where he was, they tried to keep him from leaving them. But he said, "I must preach the good news of the kingdom of God to the other towns also, because that is why I was sent." And he kept on preaching in the synagogues of Judea.

(Luke 4:40-44)

"I think we're gonna have to replace that roof
one of these days."
"Oh my. What will that cost?"
"You don't want to know."

Dave teaches Sunday school, and Candice is active in the women's ministry at church. It's hard to find people as gifted and willing as they are, and the church staff appreciates all they do for the church. They are a model family, and everyone in church looks up to them. But lately, maintaining that status as a model family has become a burden. What would happen if the house weren't perfectly decorated? If they didn't drive large, late-model cars? If the children didn't have soccer practice, piano lessons, and chess club? If they said no to a request at church? Dave and Candice don't want to think about it.

10. What do you think Jesus would have said to someone who reproached Him for going to bed before He had healed all the people in a village?

Shifting our lives from overload to margin is a spiritual battle. All the slogans, rewards, and punishments of our culture are arrayed against margin. Also, looking at our limits can be frightening: if we are limited, then we might not be able to do everything it takes to get the possessions, respect, influence, love, and security we need! The good news is that while we are limited, God is not. God has unlimited ability to give us what we need, even when we reach our limits. As we'll see in the next several sessions, living with limits is an act of real faith.

11. Find a quiet place alone, and take five minutes to be still. Imagine yourself handing over to God each area of your life in which you realize you are limited. (Are there any areas of your life in which you think you're not limited?) Hold your empty hands in your lap, palms up and open, as a gesture of letting go.

    If your mind races, sit and notice it racing without condemning yourself. See if you can allow your mind to slow down and be still as you become aware of the presence of God. Focus on your breathing, and notice whether it is deep and slow, or quick and shallow. Just notice what it is like for you to sit like this for five minutes in God's presence. Afterward, jot down a few notes about what you observed. (Did two minutes feel like ten? Did you find yourself thinking about something you need to do or should have done?)

THERE was a point in my life when, of necessity, I decided to investigate a more margined way of living. Everything seemed out of control. I remember one day in particular—a Tuesday evening in 1982. I was finishing a meeting and beginning a migraine. Meanwhile back home, my wife, Linda, went for a late evening walk. Along the dark street, her crying could be private.

My headache and Linda's crying were both manifestations of the same illness: overload. We were not only working, we were overworking. We were not only committed, we were over-committed. We were not only conscientious, we were overly conscientious. We were not only tired, we were exhausted.

Everything had become a burden: medicine and patients,

caring and serving. How could so many good things bring such pain? We were not involved in anything bad. We were meeting needs everywhere we turned. Yet life was out of control. Joy dried up and blew away. Buoyancy sank. Rest was a theoretical concept. My passion for medical practice shriveled to the size of a dehydrated pea.

I was mystified. No one had taught me about this in medical school. Nor in church. If fifteen years earlier I had written a formula for the perfect life—I had achieved it all. I had a prestigious career, a generous income, grateful patients, supportive colleagues, a great clinic, a brand new hospital, a wonderful town, a loving family, a vibrant church, and a growing faith.

But if we had such a perfect life, why was I getting all these headaches? Why was Linda crying? Why was it so hard to get out of bed in the morning?

Perhaps the turning point came when I decided to examine more closely the practice style of the Great Physician. How did Jesus care for people? He focused on the person standing in front of Him at the time. In my case, however, the person standing in front of me was often an obstacle to get around in order to get where I was going—even if that person was Linda or one of our sons.

If Jesus had chosen to live in modern America, how would He have acted? Would He have carried a pocket calendar? Can you imagine Him being paged out of the Last Supper?

There is no indication that Jesus worked twenty-hour ministry days. He went to sleep each night without having healed every disease in Israel. Neither did He minister to everybody who needed it. There were many needs he simply chose not to meet. Even when Lazarus became sick, Jesus was shockingly slow to mobilize. I would have had a helicopter there in twenty minutes. Jesus took three days.

Was He lazy or uncaring? Or did He simply understand what it meant to be human? Jesus was fully God and fully human, and His human side understood what it meant to have limits. He had to prioritize and balance in light of those limits and focus on the truly important.

When I finally understood this, life changed. Carefully, yet forcefully, Linda and I carved out margin in four areas: emotional energy, physical energy, time, and finances. As we did, ninety percent of our pain disappeared. Life came alive again. My passion for medicine returned. We remain busy, but we are no longer chronically overloaded. We still serve, teach, and help with a full investment of enthusiasm. But always within the context of limits.

....

12. To prepare to think through your budget in session 12, start recording your monthly expenses now. Create a chart with columns for groceries, clothing, housing (including home repairs), utilities, entertainment, health care, grooming (haircuts, cosmetics, razorblades, as well as gym memberships and other exercise expenses that don't fit in other categories), automobile (including insurance), and other. (See page 20-21 for an example; you can even photocopy this chart.) Many software programs make this kind of spreadsheet easy. Carry a copy of the chart with you so that you can write down what you spend as you spend it. When a new month begins, start a new chart.

In session 12 you will add up the figures in each column to find out where your money goes each month. Again, you can use software to do the math for you. If you dislike both math and learning new software, consider recruiting help from someone who is comfortable with one or the other: a friend, a coworker, even one of your children. (If you have someone else do the math, you can cross out the column headings and retitle them "Column 1" through "Column 10" for privacy.) Don't be embarrassed to ask for help! No one is good at everything.

Also, save *all* your receipts. Keep them in envelopes in chronological order (one envelope for each week).

In session 2, you will assess the ways overload is affecting you physically, emotionally, and spiritually. In sessions 3 and 4, you'll assess the sources of overload in your life. These self-inventories will help equip you to make practical, realistic plans to do something about your overload later on. If you're still struggling with the very idea that you have limits, don't worry—you'll come back to that subject in session 8.

Date	Groceries	Clothing	Housing	Utilities

Entertainment	Health Care	Grooming/Exercise	Auto	Other

For Further Study

Margin, chapters 1, 5, and 6

The Overload Syndrome, chapter 1

For Groups

Don't feel you must discuss all the questions in the session. Select those that seem most interesting or helpful to talk about.

Be sure to save time to do question 11 together—some members of your group may never have spent five minutes of silence with a group. The facilitator should keep track of the time. After your period of silence, take a few minutes to talk about what it was like to be silent and wait on God together. Talk about how you want to handle prayer in the group in future meetings.

Discuss keeping track of your expenses (question 12). This feels overwhelming to some people, and they will benefit from the moral support of the group. Some group members may have experience with budgeting and may be able to help others. One member with a spreadsheet program may be able to produce blank charts for everyone. If you want to be really serious about this, consult one of the many good books on budgeting that you can obtain from any bookstore.

Save five minutes at the end of this meeting (and every meeting) to discuss two evaluation questions:

- What went well in this meeting?
- What could we do better next time?

Notes

1. Russell D. Robinson, *An Introduction to Helping Adults Learn and Change* (Milwaukee, WI: Omnibook, 1979), p. 38. Idea credited to Howard McClusky.
2. *Resident Mental Health* (Kansas City, MO: American Academy of Family Physicians, 1988), p. 6. The human function curve is found in *Stress and Women Physicians* (New York: Springer-Verlag, 1985) by Marjorie Bowman, M.D., and Deborah I. Allen, M.D. Used by permission.
3. John Townsend, *Hiding From Love: How to Change the Withdrawal Patterns that Isolate and Imprison You* (Colorado Springs, CO: NavPress, 1991), p. 77.
4. Philippians 4:13, NKJV.
5. Genesis 2:18.

The Costs of Overload

Living without margin leaves us expended, depleted, and exhausted with no oasis in sight. Having margin, however, means that when we are drained, we have someplace to go for our healing. Overload costs.

Your objectives in this session are:

- To understand the costs of overload and the nature of stress, eustress, and distress.
- To assess ways in which you are paying the costs of overload.
- To listen closely to how a psalmist wrestles with the stresses in his life.

IN his famous story, "How Much Land Does a Man Need?," Tolstoy tells of the ambitious peasant Pakhom, who, after gaining ever greater plots of land, finally heard of a wonderful deal in a far-off country. He traveled to the land of the Bashkirs and negotiated with the village elder, who seemed a fool. The elder told Pakhom that he could have all the land he wanted for a thousand rubles a day.

Pakhom did not understand. "What kind of rate is that—a day?" he asked. "How many acres could that be?"

"We don't reckon your way. We sell by the day. However much you can walk around in one day will be yours."

When Pakhom expressed that a man can walk around much land in one day, the elder burst out laughing. "And all of it will be yours!" he replied. But there was one condition: If Pakhom didn't return to the starting point by sundown, the money would be forfeited.

Ecstatic, Pakhom spent a sleepless night. Rising at dawn, he went with the villagers to the top of a hill where the elder put down his hat. After placing his thousand rubles on top,

Pakhom began walking, digging holes along the way to mark his land. The going was easy and he thought, "I'll do another three miles and then turn left. The land's so beautiful here, it would be a pity to miss any."

Pakhom hurried throughout the morning, going out of his way to add more land. But at noon when he looked back at the hill where he had begun, it was difficult to see the people. Maybe I have gone too far, he worried, and decided he must begin to make shorter sides. As the afternoon wore on, the heat was exhausting. By now his bare feet were cut and bruised, and his legs weakened. He wanted to rest, but it was out of the question.

Pakhom struggled on, walking faster, then running. He worried that he had been too greedy and his fear made him breathless. On he ran, his shirt soaked and his throat parched. His lungs were working like a blacksmith's bellows, his heart beat like a hammer. He was terrified. "All this strain will be the death of me."

Although Pakhom feared death, he couldn't stop. *They'd call me an idiot,* he thought. When he was close enough to hear the Bashkirs cheering, he summoned his last ounce of strength and kept running. As he finally reached the hill, everything suddenly became dark—the sun had set. Pakhom groaned. He wanted to stop, but heard the Bashkirs still cheering him on. He realized that from where he was at the bottom of the hill, the sun had set—but not for those on top. Pakhom took a deep breath and rushed up the hill. Reaching the top, he saw the elder sitting by the hat, laughing his head off. Pakhom's legs gave way, and he fell forward grasping the cap.

"Oh, well done!" exclaimed the elder. "That's a lot of land you've earned yourself!"

Pakhom's worker ran up and tried to lift his master, but Pakhom was dead. The worker picked up Pakhom's spade, dug a grave, and buried him—six feet from head to heel, exactly the amount of land a man needed.

1. Read the story of Pakhom (page 23-24). Imagine you are the doctor filling out Pakhom's death certificate. What will you write under "Cause of Death"? What killed Pakhom?

Pakhom thought, *They'd call me an idiot if I stopped running now.* Who would call you an idiot if you stopped running?

2. Can you identify with Pakhom in any ways? If so, how? (If you think your situation is different, explain.)

3. Overload affects us mentally, physically, and behaviorally. It affects our relationships with other people and with God. Which of the following symptoms of overload are true in your life?

   □ I'm not having much fun.
   □ I don't have much time to care for other people's needs.
   □ I don't have much time to care for my own needs.
   □ The people closest to me (family, friends) aren't feeling loved by me.
   □ God would have to shout—and run—to get my attention.
   □ I resent people who ask for my help.

☐ I live on caffeine.

☐ I'm often irritable.

☐ I worry a lot.

☐ I take tranquilizers.

☐ I take antidepressants.

☐ I avoid people when possible.

☐ My brain is tired.

☐ I forget things frequently.

☐ I feel like things are slipping out of control.

☐ I don't expect things to get better anytime soon.

☐ I have trouble making decisions.

☐ I'm jumpy.

☐ I have trouble falling asleep at night.

☐ I wake up after just a few hours, but I don't feel rested.

☐ I hate having to get out of bed in the morning.

☐ I don't care about much anymore.

☐ I'm in survival mode.

☐ Sometimes I have so much coming at me that I go blank.

☐ I have high blood pressure.

☐ I get chest pains.

☐ My pulse races throughout much of the day.

☐ I have acid stomach.

☐ I have an ulcer.

☐ My bowels are either too loose or too tight (or some of both).

☐ My neck muscles are tense.

☐ My lower back is tense.

☐ I get headaches.

☐ I use food to calm myself.

☐ I don't care about eating.

☐ I get frequent infections.

☐ I have a rash.

☐ I get short of breath easily.

☐ My hands perspire.

☐ My hands are cold and clammy.

☐ I have a nervous tic.

☐ I clench my teeth.

☐ I lose my temper suddenly.

☐ I drive aggressively.

☐ I shop compulsively.

4. How would you summarize the effects of overload on . . .

your body?

Mentally check your body for tension right now. How are your neck muscles? See if you can relax your shoulders. How tightly are you holding your pen?

your mind?

your emotions?

your relationships with other people?

your relationship with God?

Why does overload affect us in these ways? It's helpful to understand something about stress. The late Canadian endocrinologist and "father" of stress research, Hans Selye, defined stress as "the non-specific response of the body to any demand made upon it."[1] Contrary to popular understanding, stress is not an unpleasant circumstance. Stress is our response to a circumstance. When we perceive a change in our environment, our body reacts with hormones that make us more alert, shunt blood to our brain and muscles, and provide extra oxygen and sugar for physical attack or defense. This is called the "fight or flight" response. It is useful for a physical danger or stressor, but in situations where hitting or running are inappropriate, it can be counterproductive.

Some people love the feeling of that stress response. Eustress—the constructive aspect of stress—makes us creative, efficient, and focused before a deadline. It wakes us up to deal with a midnight crisis. It gets us to peak readiness for an athletic competition. For some of us, this creative tension can even be addictive. Some employers purposely induce a stressful work environment to make employees alert and productive.

If eustress is the positive side of stress, then distress is the negative, destructive side. An excessive volume of stress (either positive or negative) is called hyperstress. The volume is important because how we deal with stress depends on how much of it we are confronted with and what type of body and personality we have. If the amounts are manageable, we can learn to avoid distress and possibly turn it into eustress. If, however, the amounts are at hyperstress levels, then stress reduction is more important than stress management. Because different people's physical and mental makeup equips them to handle different volumes of stress, their hyperstress limits will differ. Just as some people are not built to benchpress one hundred fifty pounds or throw a baseball at ninety miles an hour, so some people are not built to work on Wall Street or have three children in diapers.

A stressor, then, is some change out in the world that sets in motion our body's stress adaptation response. Stress is this physiological response to change. Dr. Selye divides the stress response into three stages: the Alarm Stage, the Resistance Stage, and the Exhaustion Stage. The Alarm Stage is the "fight or flight" phenomenon noted above. After the Alarm Stage comes the Resistance Stage, a period of vigilance and resistance. Such vigilance cannot be sustained for long, however, and the Exhaustion Stage follows.

Once we understand this sequence, we can better understand some of our behavior patterns. If we trigger the response too frequently, we will be in states of alarm or resistance too often. This overdosing on our own adrenaline has potentially serious consequences.

If the stress response is resolved in a way we view as successful, it causes no apparent damage. However, if the result is failure or frustration, it ages our cells, and it can weaken our immune system (and so cause infection or cancer) or our cardiovascular system (and so cause heart problems or stroke). "Each period of stress, especially if it results from frustrating, unsuccessful struggles, leaves some irreversible chemical scars which accumulate to constitute the signs of tissue aging," says Selye.[2] Selye's research suggests that each person has a limited amount of adaptive energy for use over a lifetime. Most of the energy expended in the stress response can be recovered through rest. But a certain amount of this energy resource may be irretrievably lost. Therefore, it's important to reserve this adaptive energy for things that matter. A car is a good analogy. Whenever we enter into a stress response, we take the car for a ride. When the gas tank runs out, we can always fill it up again. Yet each trip also puts wear and tear on the vehicle that is irreversible. This is not a reason never to drive. But it is a caution to beware of what kind of trips we take.

For some reason, physical stressors like exercise tend to produce eustress. In fact, as long as we have some control over the hard physical tasks we face, they can actually build up our bodies. (Of course, hyperstress on the body leads to injury, and forced labor is psychologically stressful.) By contrast, mental and emotional stressors—fear, chronic uncertainty, constant vigilance, frustration, and difficult mental tasks—drain our resources. In one study, a patient's blood pressure was monitored during vigorous physical exercise, and it remained normal throughout. He was then asked to subtract seven from 777 serially for three-and-one-half minutes. His blood pressure went up forty points.

Distress is nothing new—poverty, disease, and war have always led to fear, uncertainty, vigilance, and frustration. But today, even those of us who are neither poor, sick, nor in imminent danger of war are suffering stress from an unprecedented number of sources. Stress is a response to change, and we are experiencing change at faster and faster rates. Debt, hurry, and complexity cause stress. Rapidly changing job markets make us feel insecure even when we're employed. Mobility and divorce separate us from supportive relationships that would absorb distress. Study after study confirms that a healthy marriage, family, or community support structure yields better health and increased longevity. Yet the very stressors for which we need support often put intolerable pressure on those relationships.

5. In the past forty-eight hours, when have you experienced fear, chronic uncertainty, constant vigilance, frustration, or difficult mental tasks?

"Proper physical work, even if strenuous, does not absorb a great deal of the power of attention, but mental work does; so that there is no attention left over for the spiritual things that really matter. It is obviously much easier for a hard-working peasant to keep his mind attuned to the divine than for a strained office worker."[3]

6. How would you describe the connection between the experiences you named in question 5 and the symptoms of overload you listed in questions 3 and 4?

7. Studies indicate that affirming relationships are probably the single best protection against stress-induced damage to health. How would you rate the quality of the support you get from family and friends?

0	1	2	3	4	5

I get
no support
from family
and/or friends.

I get plenty
of support
from family
and/or friends.

Africa, it seems, is wealthy in margin. Here is a letter from a surgeon who spent one year there:

All things considered I would have to say that it was much healthier for me living overseas. There are stresses, of course, but of a much different type and magnitude. . . .

Although I do not consider myself a "workaholic," I do find it difficult to control the time I spend in my practice. Still, I thought I was reasonably happy until I found out how beneficial a "sabbatical" in Africa can be. . . . I wasn't exactly loafing, since I did nearly five hundred operations in that year, but I still had large amounts of free time to read, rest and play. . . .

In the absence of television, telephones and shopping centers, the inner life gets some long-needed attention. . . . I often had time for a midday nap, to eat almost all meals with my family, and to enjoy having evenings and weekends relatively free as well. With a swimming hole nearby, complete with vine swing, and surrounded by a gorgeous tropical rain forest, we could always find fun things to do. . . . We played table games, assembled puzzles together, read nearly thirty books aloud, and did creative things such as handcrafts and art. . . . The leisure time also afforded the opportunity to meditate, listen to God more, and reflect on priorities and the direction my life should take.[4]

8. What would you like about living under the circumstances described above?

A survey of *Working Mothers* readers found that 95% of people look forward to weekends to rest. But 52% were more exhausted at the end of the weekend than they were before.

9. What would you miss from your current life?

Overload harms us physically. It takes energy that we could be using for the main reasons why we are alive: loving God and loving people. Even a pastor who exhausts himself serving his congregation is not loving them well; for if he depletes himself today, he will have nothing left with which to love them tomorrow. Meanwhile, he has nothing left today with which to love his spouse, children, and God. The best reason for living within our limits is to have energy and joy with which to love for the long haul.

Into your hands I commit
my spirit;
    redeem me, O LORD, the
God of truth.
    (Psalm 31:5)

By depleting us physically, mentally, and emotionally, overload robs us spiritually. When we are overloaded, there is no space in our lives for God to act. However, the same stressors that drive us to frustration and exhaustion can, if we are wise, drive us into the arms of God. The choice is up to us: We are limited, but God is not. If we turn to God in our distress, He may not provide the energy to do superhuman work, but He will provide His presence to do a supernatural work.

10. Find a quiet place where you won't be overheard, and read Psalm 31 aloud. Listen as you read.

What words and phrases from the psalm seem to describe your situation?

What strengthening hope does the psalm offer you?

What does the psalm urge you to do?

JULIA grew up feeling she could never do enough to please her dad. Surely he was impressed when she graduated from a top university and then from a prestigious law school. Maybe he was—but he didn't seem to show it.

For some years, Julia worked eighty-hour weeks establishing herself in her legal career. But when she became interested in God, she wanted to cut back in order to make time for her spiritual life. For a while, mere forty-hour weeks allowed time for prayer and reflection, but then Julia decided to go to graduate school in theology. She volunteered at her church and on the board of a charitable organization. She left her law firm to work for a promising corporation, but soon that highly responsible position was requiring sixty or more hours of her time each week. She wanted to get married, but career, school, and volunteer work left little time for dating.

She wanted to cut back again, but by now it would be complicated to sacrifice half her income. She would have to sell her house. She could not afford a gardener, housekeeper, and restaurant meals, so while she'd spend less time at the office, she'd have to spend more time doing chores. And had she really knocked herself out all these years in law and business, only to walk away when her labor was just about to pay off? If she held on for just a few more years, she could make millions. As she turned off her cell phone after a frustrating call and hurried into church for a meeting, she wondered, *What did God want from her? What would please Him?*

11. Select a sentence from Psalm 31 that seems especially important to you. Copy it down to keep with you this week. Commit it to memory and recite it to yourself when you are in your car, in an elevator, waiting in line, or anytime you have a free moment. As you do so, invite God into the midst of your uncertainty, your vigilance, your frustration. Ask yourself, *What is God saying to me?* If any insights come to you, write them here when you get a chance.

A final word: Depression and anxiety are common effects of overload. Clinical depression is more than just feeling low for a few days. It is a physical illness in which certain brain chemicals become depleted, and it can produce sleep disturbance or oversleepiness, changes in appetite and sex drive, flatness of mood, difficulty concentrating, and other symptoms. If you think you may be clinically depressed or debilitatingly anxious, consider seeing a physician or counselor for a diagnosis.

For Further Study

Margin, chapter 4

For Groups

Check in with each other to see how tracking your expenses is going. It can be hard to get into the habit of doing this, and you may be able to share tips. This may seem like a chore, but it will yield invaluable information when you set about seeking financial margin later on.

Instead of sharing all of your symptoms in question 3, you may prefer to share only your summary thoughts in question 4. It's not necessary for everybody to know the details of one another's symptoms.

Question 7 raises the issue of a supportive place. How can your group be a supportive place?

Notes

1. Hans Selye, M.D., *Stress Without Distress* (New York: New American Library, 1974), p. 14.
2. Selye, pp. 93-94.
3. E. F. Schumacher, *Good Work* (New York: Harper and Row, 1979), p. 25.
4. Robert F. Greene, M.D., "True Confession: I Enjoyed My Year Abroad as a Short-Term Missionary," *Christian Medical and Dental Society Journal,* Winter 1990, p. 17. Reprinted by permission. The Society is a fellowship of Christian physicians and dentists representing Jesus Christ in and through medicine and dentistry (P.O. Box 5, Bristol, Tennessee 37621-0005).

The Many Faces of Overload I

When we talk about overload, most of us think first about time: We're busier than we'd like to be. Some of us think of money: We're spending more than we're earning, and we don't know where to cut back. However, the ugly truth is that we're overloaded in ways we haven't even noticed. We live with stressors that people two hundred years ago would never have dreamed of.

This is the first of two sessions designed to help you identify the sources of your overload. We have divided the material into two sessions in order to give you enough space to consider each of the ten areas carefully. Your objectives in this session are:

- To understand five areas in which people today are overloaded.
- To identify areas in which you are overloaded.

Accessibility

A major unintended consequence of the flood of accessing technologies is that soon there will be no natural excuse for being unavailable. If you are never unavailable, you have no truly private time and no true solitude. You are constantly at the mercy of interruptions. And because people know you got their message or their package, they expect an immediate response.

1. Which of the following do you own or use on a regular basis?

   ☐ A home telephone
   ☐ One or more additional home telephone lines
   ☐ A cell phone
   ☐ A pager
   ☐ A videophone and/or videoconferencing
   ☐ Voice mail

□ An answering machine

□ An answering service

□ Call Waiting telephone service

□ Three-way Calling telephone service

□ Call Forwarding telephone service

□ A menu-driven answering system

□ A fax machine

□ A desktop computer

□ A laptop computer

□ An e-mail account

□ A Web browser

□ A television

□ More than one television in your home

□ Cable TV

□ Satellite TV

□ A wireless office system

□ Overnight mail

2. Think about the items you marked in question 1. How do these contribute to your overload?

3. Do any of them reduce your overload in any ways? If so, how?

BILL is a divorced father of two children. Because he loves his kids, he gladly accepts the responsibility of paying child support, even though divorce was never his idea and child support stretches his budget to the frayed edges. On the salary of a midlevel public employee, Bill can afford a one-bedroom apartment. His ex-wife and kids live in the modest house he used to own. Hoping someday to restore his standard of living, Bill has enrolled in graduate school. He now has school two nights a week and homework on the other nights and weekends when he doesn't have his kids. At thirty-six, he's back where he was at twenty: reading textbooks at midnight while waiting for his laundry to dry.

Bill tries to attend a single's group when he can, but it's hard to date when his weekends are spent either with kids or with books. His mind is occupied every waking minute with decisions: His car has reached 200,000 miles—should he repair the air conditioning that just blew out, or get another vehicle? What payments could he push himself to afford? Can he get cheaper insurance anywhere? Should he spend the money on carryout for dinner again, or invest the time that shopping and cooking would require?

Bill goes to church. A friend invited him to a men's group, but he'd miss every other Saturday anyway because of his schedule with his kids. And frankly, on most Saturday mornings, he'd rather sleep.

Divorce almost always leads to an inefficient use of resources: supporting two households on the income and labor that should support one. It would be great if Bill could undo the past two years and put his family back together. But given that he's in this situation, he needs some help making decisions that will keep him from burning out.

Activity and Commitment

Activity overload takes away the pleasure of anticipation. Suddenly the activity is upon us, and we must rush to it. We also lack the delight of reminiscing, for we immediately move on to something new.

Friendships which formerly were solidified by shared activities are now divided by activity overload. Church congregations—worn out by mission teams, vacation Bible schools, conferences, Sunday school, holiday events, and other programs—can hardly bear another sermon that calls them to action for the sake of God's kingdom.

4. Look at your calendar for last month. As a rough, random measure of your busyness, take a look at every fourth day of that month. For each of those days, estimate the number of hours you spent doing various activities: working, running errands, taking kids to activities, volunteering, doing housework, and other activities. Include leisure events that were active rather than restful.

Day 1 _____
Day 5 _____
Day 9 _____
Day 13 _____
Day 17 _____
Day 21 _____
Day 25 _____
Day 29 _____

5. Now look at the coming week. For each day of the week, write down how many hours of activity you have scheduled.

Day 1 _____
Day 2 _____
Day 3 _____
Day 4 _____
Day 5 _____
Day 6 _____
Day 7 _____

6. How do you think your schedule affects your sense of overload?

Change

As we saw in session 2, stress is an internal, bodily adaptation to any change in our environment. Some level of stress and change is good for us; otherwise, we would be bored and contribute little to the world. However, the past fifty years have seen an unprecedented increase in the rate of change in the world. That is, not only are things changing faster than they used to, they are changing faster this decade than last decade, and they will probably change faster next year than this year.

7. In the past fifteen years, how many times have you . . .

changed your residence? _____
changed churches? _____
changed jobs? _____
changed your kids' schools? _____
changed health insurance? _____
changed doctors? _____
changed marital status? _____
changed whom you live with? _____
lost a loved one to death? _____
learned a new computer program? _____
learned to use a new technological device? _____

8. How do you think all this change has affected you?

9. One negative effect of change is the undermining of support systems. When we, our family, and our friends move often, it's hard to form deep bonds with people whom we know will be around through the ups and downs of our lives. When a marriage dissolves or our kids change schools, the fabric of relationships is

The average American occupies 12 to 13 residences in a lifetime, twice as many as the average person in Britain or France, and four times as many as the typical Irish.[3]

On average, women in the United States change jobs ever 5.8 years, and men every 7.6 years.[4]

Your local grocery store may contain:
184 different kinds of breakfast cereal
125 kinds of yogurt
177 kinds of salad dressing.

torn. How has change affected the quality of the support system—family and friends—that you currently have available to you?

Choice and Decision

Which of the two hundred fifty varieties of toothpaste do you buy? Mint? Gel? Tartar control regular? Pump or tube? North Americans love choices. And progress works by differentiating our environment (as we'll explore further in session 4). Progress relentlessly hands us more choices, and each choice requires a decision. Nobody used to have to decide whether to keep loved ones alive with machines after they lose consciousness. Nobody had to be an expert in shopping for cars, selecting insurance, investing for retirement, negotiating the tax assessment of one's home, and choosing the right preschool for one's children. Should you pay extra for antilock brakes? An extended warranty? An antitheft device?

All of these decisions require analysis of information, often complex information. Leonard Laster, M.D. complains that his postgraduate training in analytical mathematics is inadequate for calculating the best long-distance phone plan for his needs. Most of us know we make many decisions without fully thinking through the options just because all that thinking is exhausting. It's no wonder we long for an easy formula for knowing God's will—if God would make even half of our major decisions for us, we would sleep better at night.

10. What choices in your life feel especially difficult or burdensome to you (if any)?

11. What decisions do you avoid making (if any)?

"While choices multiply, we stay pretty much the same. Our bodies and minds remain the bottleneck through which choice must pass. We still have the same brains our forebears did, still only twenty-four hours a day to use them. . . . The opportunity to choose among many options is, of course, a good thing. But maybe you can have too much of a good thing?"[5]

12. In what areas of your life do you prefer routine?

13. In what areas of life do you prefer to make new choices often?

Progress has given us more information in the past thirty years than in all the previous 5000 years combined.[6]

Information

The typical business manager is said to read one million words per week.[7] Such situations have spawned a new syndrome, Information Fatigue Syndrome (IFS). Symptoms of IFS include anxiety, self-doubt, paralysis of analytical capacity, a tendency to blame others, time-wasting, and in some cases illness. When we know that in order to make good decisions we would have to digest many times more information than we can hope even to glance at, we may feel set up for failure and respond with the feelings and behaviors of IFS.

14. How many magazines, newspapers, and journals arrive at your home and office each month? (If this figure is more than twenty-five, you can estimate.)

15. To be really up to date in your field, about how many hours per day do you think you would have to read or listen to new information?

16. In an average week, about how many hours do you spend reading, watching, or listening to news reports and/or newsmagazine TV shows?

17. How do you think information overload affects you?

18. What thoughts or feelings are going through your mind after assessing these five areas of your life?

19. What would you like to say to God right now?

IF starving, we need not be told we lack food. If bankrupt, we need not be told we need money. Why, then, when we so desperately need margin in our lives, is it necessary to *explain* our need for it? Why don't we understand it by instinct?

Some burdens and pains in life are visible while others are not. "Visible" means they can be perceived with one of the five senses, quantified, or measured. For example, if you smash your finger, you do not have to guess what hurts or why. Physical pains are obvious. Financial pains, likewise, are usually visible. If the credit-card statement reveals a three-thousand-dollar debt, the source of your distress is not obscure.

Other pains, however, cannot be perceived by the senses or measured in the same way. They are semivisible. Emotional, psychological, social, relational, and spiritual pains often fit this description. The pain is real, but the details of cause and effect are hard to sort out. It often requires months of counseling or introspection to clarify wounds in these areas.

In the same way, margin is semivisible. Living without it does not cause a sensory pain, but instead a deep-seated subjective ache. Because the ache and heaviness are only semivisible, the pain of marginless living is hard for us to talk about. We feel guilty and weak if we complain. We feel vulnerable to the slings and arrows of the contemptuously stoic. It is hard to justify our inner pains when we don't even

> know what the enemy is. We lack a vocabulary to speak of it. Only when it manifests in something obvious like heart disease, alcohol abuse, divorce, or bankruptcy do we label it, and then we use the name of the result (heart disease) rather than the cause (marginless living). It is far better, though, to begin treasuring margin before health or marriage collapses.

For Further Study

The Overload Syndrome, chapters 3, 4, 5, 6, and 10

For Groups

Share the highlights of your answers to questions 1-17. You needn't comb through every detail, but tell the group about those issues that seemed most significant to you. Which ones stood out as problem areas for you? Which ones had you not thought of before? Which ones seem most connected to your feelings of stress?

Discuss your answers to question 18. Are you feeling unburdened because you've identified some of the sources of your sense of overload? Or are you feeling overwhelmed because solutions seem difficult?

Check in on your task of keeping track of your expenses. How is it going?

Use question 19 as a basis of prayer for each other.

Notes

1. James M. Cerletty, M.D., "I'm Dying of Easy Accessibility," *The Journal of Family Practice,* 42 No. 4, April 1996, p. 335.
2. J. Grant Howard, *Balancing Life's Demands: A New Perspective on Priorities* (Portland, OR: Multnomah, 1983), p. 144.
3. Rodger Doyle, "House to House," *The Atlantic Monthly,* March 1993, p. 95.
4. "Longer Lives, Less Cash," *U.S. News & World Report,* 12 August 1996, p. 14.
5. Robert Kanigel, "Too Much of a Good Thing?" *Washington Post National Weekly Edition,* 12 January 1998, p. 25
6. Peter Large, *Information Anxiety: What to Do When Information Doesn't Tell You What You Need to Know* (New York: Bantam, 1990), p. 35.
7. David Shenk, *Data Smog: Surviving the Information Glut* (New York: HarperEdge, 1977), pp. 30-31.

The Many Faces of Overload II

In session 3 you examined five areas of life in which you may be overloaded. You'll look at five more in this session. Your objectives this time are similar to those last time, but with one addition:

- To understand five more areas in which people today are overloaded.
- To identify areas in which you are overloaded.
- To commit to making space in your life for God to act.

This last objective is crucial. Of all the reasons to have margin in your life (physical and mental health, the ability to love others), space for God is the one that rules over all the rest. You may come to the end of this session and have no idea how—in practical terms—to make this kind of space. That's okay. Sessions 5 through 12 will help you identify how. The key here, though, is *How badly do you want it?*

First, however, take a look at five more areas of overload that may leave you breathless. If you feel stressed just answering the questions, pause and pray. Imagine yourself relaxing into God's arms for a moment.

Hurry

Time crunch. Fast food. Rush hour. Frequent flyer. Expressway. Overnight delivery. Rapid transit. Sprint. Quicken. DayRunner. SlimFast. Our society highly values speed, and things just keep moving faster and faster.

1. In what areas of life (if any) do you enjoy speed?

2. In what areas of your life is speed or hurry a burden?

Media

"At MTV, we don't shoot for the 14-year-olds, we own them." [1]

Research has demonstrated that we store three trillion "videotape" images in our brain by the time we are thirty years old. But we have no volitional control over selective forgetting. Once the images of sex, violence, or empty sentimentality are there, we must live with the consequences of that video imprint.

The same is true of the auditory imprint of song lyrics, movie dialogue, and news. If we bombard our ears with a philosophy of "luv lite" or nihilism, it will shape our values and expectations about life.

3. Which of these effects of media saturation have you experienced?

☐ I am accustomed to seeing people terrorized, maimed, and killed.

☐ I am accustomed to hearing profanity.

☐ I am accustomed to sexual infidelity.

☐ I feel lonely or otherwise uncomfortable without music or television playing.

☐ When I feel sad, lonely, or bored, I turn to media to pick me up.

☐ I don't like going on vacation or retreat without a source of news or media entertainment.

☐ I'm cynical about politics.

☐ I rarely get much silence in my life.

Debt

In 1997, U.S. consumer debt stood at 1.4 trillion dollars.[2] A trillion anything is hard to imagine, but try to conceive of a million households, each of which is 1.4 million dollars in debt. Or maybe ten million households, each of which owes $140,000. Bankruptcy is largely a white, middle-class phenomenon. These people, who have pushed spending to the limit to pay for a house, furnishings, a nice car, a work wardrobe, and the needs of children, are suddenly pushed over the edge by a crisis, such as the loss of a job, a divorce, or an illness. With no margin for the unexpected, their house of cards tumbles.

4. How many credit cards do you (and your spouse, if you're married) currently own?

5. Find all of your most recent credit card statements. Find your car payment, if you have one. Find any statements for outstanding loans. How much money do you currently owe, not counting your home mortgage?

6. If you couldn't bring yourself to do the math for question 5, why is that?

7. How do you think debt affects your sense of overload, if at all?

Possessions

Years ago in Siam, if the king had an enemy he wanted to torment, it was easy: give him a white elephant. The receiver of this gift was now obligated into oblivion. Any gift from the king obviously had to be cared for—it could not be given away without causing offense. Additionally, a white elephant was considered sacred and thus required the best nourishment and protection. Soon the extreme costs of caring for the gift drove the king's enemy to destitution.

Today we go out of our way to acquire possessions that require storage space and upkeep. We overwork or go into debt to afford them. When they drive us to destitution, we don't even have a king to blame. There is only those darned Joneses with whom we are trying to keep up.

The *Catalog of Catalogs* lists more than twelve thousand catalogs from which to order.

8. You've been keeping track of expenses for several weeks now. What patterns are emerging?

9. In what ways do possessions contribute to your overload?

RUSSELL likes stimulating work—he always has. But lately he's had trouble coming down at night. He lives on an adrenaline buzz. He mainlines coffee. At 1:00 a.m. he stares at the ceiling.

The truth is, the relentless pressure to perform at work is taking its toll. At twenty-five, he loved the take-no-prisoners attitude. But these days he's not quite as resilient after a ten-hour flight or a sixteen-hour day. He's not even close to getting old, but already he's having dreams of wolves devouring those in the pack who become too weak to keep up.

Russell doesn't want to change jobs. He just wants to shift this job down a notch. Unfortunately, his CEO is one of those guys who came installed with extra batteries. Russell is afraid that if he suggests cutting back to a sixty-hour week, his commandant will give him one of "those" looks.

Restoring margin to his life will require Russell to take some serious risks and make a significant shift in his perspective. He risks plateauing his upward mobility or even losing his job to someone younger and hungrier. So much of his self-respect is tied up in achievement at work that losing status there feels like losing a piece of his manhood. For Russell, spiritual growth will include seeking a sense of manhood from being an involved husband, father, and child of God. It will take creativity and determination to learn to live on only moderate doses of that adrenaline rush.

In 1995, U.S. workers averaged 1,896 working hours, outpacing all other industrialized countries, including Japan.[4]

Work

Work is obviously God-ordained. A life without meaningful work is a tragic life. But work overload is a different matter. One in six workers in the United States admits that he or she thinks about quitting on a weekly basis.[3] The proliferation of labor-saving devices has made us more productive, so that our (economic) standard of living is higher, but although the average hours people worked declined from 1850 to 1920, it has been rising again since 1980 at roughly the same rate. The forty-hour workweek is a thing of the past.

10. How many hours do you work in an average week?

11. Do you think your job is a significant source of your sense of overload? If so, in what ways?

Studies have shown that somewhere between fifty and sixty hours of work per week, productivity and efficiency begin to reverse. (Recall figure 1 on page 10.) One study in England revealed that at sixty hours a week, performance declined by twenty-five percent.

12. Which of these have you experienced?

☐ Decreased productivity as I exceed my effective number of work hours without rest
☐ A repetitive strain injury, such as Carpal Tunnel Syndrome
☐ Sleep disturbance because of irregular work hours or thinking about work at night
☐ Inadequate time with family because of work schedule
☐ Pressure from my workplace to make work my top priority

Making Space for God

13. As you review the sources of overload in this session and the previous one, which ones do you think are especially significant in your life?

14. Read the quotation from Henri Nouwen in the sidebar. What goes through your mind when you think about making space in your life for God to act?

"In the spiritual life, the word discipline means 'the effort to create some space in which God can act.' Discipline means to prevent everything in your life from being filled up. Discipline means that somewhere you're not occupied, and certainly not preoccupied. In the spiritual life, discipline means to create that space in which something can happen that you hadn't planned or counted on."
—Henri J. M. Nouwen[5]

15. Make Nouwen's words the focus of your prayer this week. You might even copy them onto a card so that you can read and think about them while you are sitting at stoplights. What would it take for you to make real space in your life for God to act? What do you think it might require of you? What might it cost you?

16. What are the potential benefits of making space in your life for God?

17. Are you ready to commit to finding ways to make that space? Are you ready to face the cost? What moves you to say yes or no?

Perhaps you still have two minds about doing what it would take to make space for God. In sessions 5 and 6 you will begin to look at the forces in your world that push you toward overload even though it costs you so much—forces like progress, the success ethic, and expectations. These sessions will help you put your finger on why you may have difficulty just saying "no" to overload.

For Further Study

The Overload Syndrome, chapters 7, 9, 11, 12, and 13

For Groups

Discuss the highlights of your answers to questions 1-12. Talk about how it felt to answer these questions and what you learned about yourself from doing so.

Is there any connection in your life between overload regarding debt, possessions, and work? For example, accumulating more stuff can mean more debt, and more debt requires more work to pay off the debt. Does your life reflect this pattern?

Save at least twenty minutes for questions 13-17. This commitment is key, but no one should be pressured into saying yes to it. There are strong reasons why we resist making this commitment, and the next several sessions will address those reasons. End your meeting with some time of honest prayer about where each of you is on this score.

Notes

1. Bob Pittman, former MTV chairman.
2. Fred Vogelsein, "Giving Credit Where Credit Is Undue," *U.S. News & World Report*, 31 March 1997, p. 52.
3. Cindy Hall and Julie Stacey, "Quitting Time," *USA Today*, 10 February 1997, p. 1B.
4. Hans J. Heine, International Editor, Institut der Deutschen Wirtschaft, *Industrie Anzeiger,* 1996, p. 7.
5. Henri J. M. Nouwen, "Moving from Solitude to Community to Ministry," *Leadership,* Spring 1995, p. 81.

Progress and Success

When we assess the costs of overload, we may wonder why we tolerate it. Why not just walk away from the things that exceed our limits? But then, when we look at all those sources of overload, we may feel helpless. *I have to be accessible,* we think. *I have to work. I need my possessions and my television time. I have to make all those decisions.* Cutting back in any of those areas doesn't look like an option. For the next several sessions, we will zero in on the forces that make us believe we can't reduce our load.

The external, cultural force that most strongly wars against margin in our lives is progress. Most of us have been raised to believe progress is good, so it will be helpful to examine the downside of progress. Allied with progress is the concept of success. What does it mean to succeed in life or be "better off" than we were ten years ago?

Your objectives in this session are:

- To understand how our culture defines progress and success in ways that sabotage margin.
- To evaluate the premises of progress and success in light of biblical values.
- To decide the extent to which you want to continue to serve our culture's views of progress and success.

Progress means proceeding to a higher state of development. "The idea of progress holds that mankind has advanced in the past . . . is now advancing, and will continue to advance through the foreseeable future," explains historian Robert Nisbet. "From at least the early nineteenth century until a few decades ago, belief in the progress of mankind, with Western civilization in the vanguard, was virtually a universal religion on both sides of the Atlantic."[1] Progress was thought to be automatic. Thus, saying we had lived from 1950 to 1970 was synonymous with saying we had progressed two decades. The flow of progress was assumed to be inherently positive.

Under this philosophy, modernization was given the positive spin term "development." It was believed that we were moving toward finding remedies for each disease, eliminating poverty, and finding new technologies to eliminate energy shortages. Yet in the past two decades we have learned to doubt the religion of progress as it has brought us progressively more serious drug abuse, sexually transmitted diseases, violent crime, social breakdown, environmental degradation, national debt, and foreign debt.

There are two fatal flaws in the philosophy of progress. One is the law of unintended consequences. "Many of the crises of the present have *positive* origins," explain scientists Mesarovic and Pestel in *Mankind at the Turning Point*. "They are consequences of actions that were, at their genesis, stimulated by man's best intentions." [2] Burning fossil fuels greatly advances our comfort and mobility, but it also produces acid rain. Mobility enables us to find better jobs and live in interesting places, but it also separates us from our families and plants us in temporary neighborhoods of strangers. Housing projects were supposed to help the poor, not ghettoize them in war zones. Suburbs were supposed to give middle-class people the good life, not condemn them to grueling commutes.

The second flaw in progress is that Americans and Europeans have defined it in terms of money, technology, and education. Those are valuable things, but *none of them serves our transcendent needs*. Most Americans believe that if they earn a Ph.D., get a raise, buy a new house, or upgrade to a faster computer, they are "better off." But what about the depressed schoolteacher or the recently divorced executive with a suicidal adolescent daughter or the octogenarian being force-fed in the nursing home? By what economic and cognitive parameters do we measure their "progress"?

In our enthusiasm to improve material and cognitive performance, we have neglected social, emotional, and spiritual contributions to our well-being. If you're making more money but your family is crumbling, are you better off? If your technology is many times faster and smaller than it was two years ago, but your anxiety and indecisiveness have increased, is that progress? Should you devote the next ten years to getting smarter or to getting wiser?

We can ask the same questions about the term "success" as we can about progress. To what extent will we measure success by money, material productivity, and education? To what extent will we measure success by relational intimacy, emotional health, and spiritual depth?

Hearing that Jesus had silenced the Sadducees, the Pharisees got together. One of them, an expert in the law, tested him with this question: "Teacher, which is the greatest commandment in the Law?"

Jesus replied: "'Love the Lord your God with all your heart and with all your soul and with all your mind.' This is the first and greatest commandment. And the second is like it: 'Love your neighbor as yourself.' All the Law and the Prophets hang on these two commandments."

(Matthew 22:34-40)

1. What makes you feel valuable, worthwhile, or significant?
   (Check as many items as apply to you.)

   ☐ Earning money
   ☐ Making someone else feel loved
   ☐ Doing a good job on a task
   ☐ Receiving praise from others
   ☐ Getting my way in a conflict
   ☐ Helping others solve a problem
   ☐ Expressing my creativity
   ☐ Remembering that God created me in the image of Himself
   ☐ Having academic degrees
   ☐ Having professional expertise
   ☐ Knowing that I am a child of God
   ☐ Being with people who love me
   ☐ Other: _____
   ☐ Other: _____
   ☐ Other: _____

2. Read Matthew 22:34-40. What does Jesus say life is about?

Some people understand Jesus to be saying that the meaning of life mainly involves what *we do for God*. The apostle John corrected this misunderstanding when he wrote, "This is love: not that we loved God, but that he loved us and sent his Son as an atoning sacrifice for our sins" (1 John 4:10). What *we do* is a response to what *God has always been doing*. In fact, one important facet of loving God is gratefully and fully receiving the love God gives to us.

> Blessed is the man who finds wisdom,
> the man who gains understanding,
> for she is more profitable than silver
> and yields better returns than gold.
> She is more precious than rubies;
> nothing you desire can compare with her.
> Long life is in her right hand;
> in her left hand are riches and honor.
> Her ways are pleasant ways,
> and all her paths are peace.
> She is a tree of life to those who embrace her;
> those who lay hold of her will be blessed.
> (Proverbs 3:13-18)

3. How would really accepting Jesus' answer to the meaning of life affect the way you answered question 1?

"Therefore I tell you, do not worry about your life, what you will eat or drink; or about your body, what you will wear. Is not life more important than food, and the body more important than clothes? Look at the birds of the air; they do not sow or reap or store away in barns, and yet your heavenly Father feeds them. Are you not much more valuable than they?"
Matthew 6:25-26

4. Think about this progression: data—information—knowledge—wisdom. Which of these four occupies most of your mental energy in a typical day? Which gets the least attention from you?

most _____

least _____

5. According to Proverbs 3:13-18, how would a smart person prioritize those four items?

6. Look back over your life and think about the "progress" or "success" you have had in each of the following areas. What evidence do you see in your life of success or lack of success in each area?

acquisition of money and possessions

productivity (making worthwhile things; performing worth-while services)

education (gaining degrees; learning data, information, and knowledge)

wisdom (understanding how the world works; understanding what's important in life and how to get or do it)

Beware of success. It breeds increased expectations. "We not only have successes, we become our successes. And the more we allow our accomplishments . . . to become the criteria of our self-esteem, the more we are . . . never sure if we will be able to live up to the expectations which we created by our last successes. In many people's lives, there is a nearly diabolic chain in which their anxieties grow according to their successes."[3]

relationships (building solid, intimate relationships where others know and value who you really are; loving others deeply and actively)

emotional depth and richness (ability to feel a broad spectrum of feelings from sorrow to joy; ability to understand and respond to others' feelings; freedom from anxiety, depression, and rage)

"People can become psychologically trapped by their own success as they race to keep up with the rising expectations bred by each new achievement. With each success they raise their level of difficulty, climbing up a ladder of subgoals, moving faster, raising aspirations and at some point reaching the limit of their capacity.

"At this point, successful performance becomes difficult and people begin to lose more often than they win. Their resources are squeezed to the utmost. The business executive, promoted beyond a level of just manageable difficulty, ends up being held together by a thin paste of alcohol, saunas, and antibiotics."[4]

spiritual depth (a consistent sense of God's realness; awe and enjoyment of God; freedom from life-controlling problems like addiction, arrogance, lust for power; a value system in line with the kingdom of God)

7. In what ways are you better off than you were ten years ago?

"We are frequently asked if it is possible to 'have it all'—a full, satisfying personal life and a full and satisfying, hardworking professional one. Our answer is: NO. . . . Excellence is a high cost item."[5]

8. In what ways are you not better off—making no progress or even regressing?

9. To what extent do your areas of success match the areas that you most value and the areas that give you the most sense of being valuable?

10. How do you think God defines success?

11. What thoughts and feelings go through your mind when you think about the areas of your success and lack of success?

Failure is an almost unthinkable concept for many of us. If we aren't succeeding, then we're failing, and that means we are worthless. Success = value. Failure = worthlessness. Those are laws of our world as certain as $E=mc^2$. However, in the kingdom of God, lack of success— and even failure—are opportunities to receive grace. Blessed are the poor in spirit—the spiritual failures—for the kingdom of the heavens is available right now even to them. In Matthew 5:3, Jesus is not saying that being poor in spirit is a way to earn our tickets into the kingdom of heaven. He is saying that *even* those of us who have been bounding forward on the wrong road and suddenly realize we are spiritual failures—even we can start participating in the life of God right now because the King of the kingdom is extending His hand to us. It is not too late to stop climbing the wrong mountain. We can take a detour and start following the King, learning to live by His ways.

"WHAT do you really want?" Brian keeps asking himself that question. If Jesus appeared in the room and told him he could have either a four-bedroom house or an intimate knowledge of the Father—but not both—which would he actually choose? Part of him thinks if he knew God intimately, nothing else would matter. But he knows his behavior says he's choosing the house. Why else would he be working so hard to move up in his company and spending so much of his free time visiting Home Depot or working in the yard? Maybe because knowing God seems a lot more elusive than paying a mortgage and mowing a lawn, he's going for what seems the more attainable goal.

What do the kids really need? Do they need to see their dad in the evening, or do they each need their own rooms? What about when they're teenagers? Will they say, "We wish you'd worked late every night so we wouldn't have to share a bedroom"? Can you raise a child today who would rather be rich in parents than in space and stuff? Brian wishes he could have a guarantee that if he chooses to give his children more time and less money, they will be happy. In part, his motive is selfish: he wants his kids to say to him when they're twenty, "Way to go, Dad! You did the right thing!" But more than that, he wants them to grow up healthy and joyful, deprived of nothing essential to their well-being. That's what he really wants, more than just a house (and maybe more than knowing God, if the truth be told). But what is essential to their well-being?

Sorting out everybody's wants and needs is so complicated. Jesus said, "Seek first the kingdom of God, and the rest will follow." Does that mean that seeking God first would make Brian's other questions clearer?

12. As you look ahead to the next ten years of your life, if you had to settle for less material and cognitive progress in order to make more progress in relationships, emotions, wisdom, and spirituality, would that be a worthwhile tradeoff for you? Explain your reasoning.

"Driven people operate on the precept that a reputation for busyness is a sign of success and personal importance. Thus they attempt to impress people with the fullness of their schedule. They may even express a high level of self-pity, bemoaning the 'trap' of responsibility they claim to be in, wishing aloud that there was some possible release from all that they have to live with. But just try to suggest a way out!"[6]

13. Set aside ten minutes for silence alone with God. Sit comfortably, and lay your hands open, palms up, in your lap or on your knees. Let this be a gesture of offering up to God the years of your life so far, with areas of success and areas of unsuccess. As you sit with God, you don't have to do or say anything. Try to receive God's compassion and forgiveness for the misdirections and failures of your life so far. It may be that it's harder for you to forgive yourself than for God to forgive you. If you find it helpful, reflect on Jesus' words in Matthew 5:3: "Blessed are the poor in spirit, for theirs is the kingdom of heaven."

At the end of ten minutes, thank God for His compassion, and thank Him also for the remaining years of your life in which you have a chance to change direction if necessary or go further in the direction of the kingdom of God. Thank Him for the astounding things He plans to do in you and through you for the rest of your life.

For Further Study
Margin, chapter 2
The Overload Syndrome, chapter 2

For Groups

Sessions 3 and 4 can be discouraging in that they confront you with the load you are carrying. Session 5 can be discouraging in another way: it confronts you with the goals you have been pursuing and your level of success at reaching them. Success is so important in our society that facing our areas of little or no success can feel devastating. And realizing that we have been succeeding at goals God doesn't care about and failing at goals God cares very much about can feel even more devastating. Hence, it's important to use your group meeting as a time for people to unload any shame they may be carrying. If people feel ashamed of not being successful as the world accounts success, that is *illegitimate* shame. Not living up to the world's standards is not a sin. Talk about feelings of illegitimate shame: Whose opinion (your father's, your college classmates', your coworkers' . . .) seems to matter so much? Why does that person's or persons' opinion matter to you?

On the other hand, if people feel ashamed of not living up to God's standard of success, that is *legitimate* shame. This kind of failure *is* sin. The answers to sin are confession, repentance, and forgiveness. Talk about feelings of legitimate shame. How have you fallen short in the areas that matter to God? Are you committed to change? Are you willing to receive forgiveness and go on? God's answer to the ashamed sinner is, "Neither do I condemn you. . . . Go now and leave your life of sin" (John 8:11).

In addition to this conversation about feelings, be sure everyone is clear on how God defines success (questions 2, 3, 5, 10). How did each of you put into words your answers to question 10? Any disagreements?

Talk about what it was like to do the exercise in question 13. Close your meeting with a time of prayer regarding your goals for success in life.

Notes

1. Robert Nisbet, *History of the Idea of Progress* (New York: Basic Books, 1980), pp. 4-5,7.
2. Mihajlo Mesarovic and Eduard Pestel, *Mankind at the Turning Point: The Second Report of the Club of Rome* (New York: New American Library, 1974), p. 11.
3. Henri J. M. Nouwen, *Out of Solitude: Three Meditations on the Christian Life* (Notre Dame, IN: Ave Maria Press, 1974), pp. 18-19.
4. Gilbert Brim, "Losing and Winning," *Psychology Today*, September 1988, p. 52.
5. Thomas J. Peters & Nancy Austin, *A Passion for Excellence* (New York: Random House, 1985).
6. Gordon MacDonald, *Ordering Your Private World* (Nashville: Oliver-Nelson, 1985), p. 36.

Expectations

Our happiness and contentment are dependent on the expectations we bring to an experience. As progress gives us more and more benefits, it raises expectations. This, in turn, often makes it harder to find the happiness and contentment we seek. Progress has shown us that life *can* be improved. But it has also taught us to expect that life *will* be improved. Moreover, our expectations tend to rise faster than the improvements.

Happiness depends on expectation, not on actual improvement. If, for example, we expect a car and receive two cars, we are ecstatic. But if we expect three cars and receive two, we are crushed. In each case, we received two cars. The emotional result, however, was polar opposite. Likewise, if we expect an apartment and receive a house, we are thrilled. But if we receive an older home when we expected a new one with a master bath and three-car garage, we feel poor and deprived.

We are also burdened by others' expectations. Everywhere we turn, we find messages telling us we are expected to be smart (or at least educated), beautiful, fashionable, and athletic; to drive a nice car; to live in a beautiful home that is always picked up; to own things at least as nice as the neighbors'; and to be perfect spouses and parents. These messages warn us that if we don't meet these expectations, we will be disgraced and shunned.

Your objectives in this session are:

- To identify your and others' expectations about your life.
- To understand how these expectations affect the decisions you make about margin.
- To understand how the kind of person you are affects the expectations that are reasonable for you.

One day when I was working my rotating shift at the Student Health Center in our university, my car was ticketed: "Please move your car. This spot is reserved for the physician." Why did the officer write this note if not for a cultural expectation that an M.D. would not drive a car like mine?

1. Do you sense expectations about the car you should be driving? If so, from where do those expectations come?

   □ The media
   □ Coworkers
   □ Friends
   □ My kids
   □ My spouse
   □ My parents
   □ Inside myself

2. What sort of car do those people expect you to own?

3. What kind of home do you expect you should have? (Consider size, value, location, amenities, and whether you own or rent.)

Over the past forty years, Americans have doubled the square footage of their homes, even though families are smaller.

4. From where do you get your expectation of the kind of home you should have?

5. What kinds of clothes are you expected to wear . . .

   for work?

   for leisure?

6. What do you expect your annual income should be?

7. On what basis do you arrive at that figure?

8. How do you expect your career to go?

JACOB'S misfortune is that his older sister married a business genius. Mark, Jacob's brother-in-law, was running a company by the time he was twenty-eight. How many times has Jacob heard his mother say, "Why can't you be more like Mark?"

Mark is a deacon in his church and owns three cars. Mark has taken Jacob's parents to Hawaii. Mark and Julie have two darling children. Jacob, on the other hand, is working in a job he hates in order to afford one car and a house that's a quarter the size of Mark's. Even when his mother isn't there, he hears her voice: "If only you'd gotten into _____ College." "It's too bad you have to settle for that jacket. Mark's jackets fit him so well."

Jacob's wife, Caroline, keeps saying, "When are you going to stop trying to live up to your mother's standard of who you should be? Did God retire and leave His throne to her?" Of course, Caroline has a point. Jacob's mother does occupy the position either of God or the Devil in his mind. But he doesn't like having Caroline point it out. He really doesn't.

Historically speaking, retirement has been possible for only a generation or two in only a few countries. For most of history—and even now in most of the world—only the very rich could afford to spend any portion of their lives not working full time. And when the retirement age was set at sixty-five back in the 1930s, life expectancy was such that most people were unlikely to live more than a few years beyond retirement. The notion that a middle-class person might expect to spend two decades or more in idleness would have been inconceivable except in Europe and North America after 1960.

9. At what age (if ever) do you expect to be able to retire?

10. What do you expect from health care? (For instance, do you expect to be pain-free? Do you expect to be protected from major debilitating illness?)

11. What level of physical and athletic ability do you expect to have ten years from now?

12. What level of physical attractiveness (smooth skin, toned shape, thick hair, and so on) do you expect to have five years from now?

13. To what degree do you expect to be free from mental and emotional suffering?

Researchers have studied what is called "the disclosure effect." If I have a frustration inside and am able to reveal my heart to a safe friend, simply "disclosing" the problem will improve my well-being in measureable ways. It is not necessary for my friend to fix the problem—all he or she has to do is listen.

14. What do you expect from your marriage partner (or potential partner, if you are single)?

15. What do you expect from your children (if you have or are planning to have children)?

16. What expectations about your participation in church activities do you sense from . . .

other people?

yourself?

CHILDREN today daily watch five hours of television, including one hour of commercials. Avon sells Barbie cosmetics. One toiletry manufacturer is marketing solid deodorant for seven-year-olds, even though such children have no physiological need for the product until at least age eleven.

"Advertisers are focusing more and more on the emerging market of 'people who do only what they want to do,'" observes columnist John Leo, "that is, people who yearn to be completely free of all restraint, expectations, and responsibilities." Burger King offers, *Sometimes you gotta break the rules.* A shoe company promises their shoe *conforms to your foot so you don't have to conform to anything.* Says Nike, *We are all hedonists and we want what feels good. That's what makes us human.* "The point here," explains Leo, "is that while everyone is aghast at blatant sex, violent movies, and gangsta rap, the ordinary commercial messages of corporate America are probably playing a more subversive role." [1]

Advertising tells us to ignore society's expectations of appropriate behavior (show up at work on time, say please and thank you, be responsible and committed). At the same time, it tells us to be obsessively concerned with society's expectations (be a cool, hip nonconformist; have no body odor; look pretty and rich).

17. Look back over these expectations. Which ones most affect your contentment with what you have now?

☐ Home
☐ Clothes
☐ Income
☐ Career
☐ Retirement
☐ Health care
☐ Physical and athletic ability
☐ Physical attractiveness
☐ Freedom from emotional and mental suffering
☐ Marriage partner
☐ Children
☐ Church activities

It is three times as hard to get out of debt as to get into it, and it sentences us to a lower lifestyle in the future.

18. What other strong expectations do you have about life?

19. How are your expectations affected by what other people have (people you know, people you hear about, or characters on television)?

IN the 1950s, people used to try to keep up with the Joneses, who typically lived next door and made about the same amount of money. However, economist Juliet B. Schor describes "the new consumerism," in which we now compare ourselves not to our neighbors (we may not even know our neighbors), but to our coworker in the corner office, to celebrities, and to fashionable television characters. Schor estimates that every extra hour per week spent watching television correlates with a $208 increase in annual spending. Most Americans spend money on "visibles," such as cars, clothes, and home furnishings, while scrimping on "invisibles," such as retirement savings and college funds. Women are more likely to buy expensive lipsticks than expensive facial cleansers, not because expensive lipsticks are better quality, but because women often apply lipstick in public and don't want to be seen using a cheap brand.[2]

20. Are you more inclined to compare your life to the lives of people who have more than you or to the lives of people who have less? Why do you suppose that's the case?

21. How do you think the expectations you have listed affect your overload in these areas?

    work

    activities

    debt

"Do not store up for yourselves treasures on earth, where moth and rust destroy, and where thieves break in and steal. But store up for yourselves treasures in heaven, where moth and rust do not destroy, and where thieves do not break in and steal. For where your treasure is, there your heart will be also."
   (Matthew 6:19-21)

"In repentance and rest is
your salvation,
    in quietness and trust is
your strength. . . ."
    (Isaiah 30:15)

possessions

One thing that influences our expectations and their validity is the personality and physical makeup with which God has uniquely designed each one of us. Our culture values productivity, so many of us expect ourselves (and those around us) to be like the most productive people we know. We might call those in the top ten percent of productivity Highly Productive People (HPP). They get by on less sleep, always seem to have energy to spare, rise to the top of organizations, and lead the charge to the future. They do much of the work, make most of the decisions, develop most of the new products, and create most of the wealth that the rest of us depend on. They are persistent—they have a special talent for putting in long hours, staying focused, and still maintaining energy and passion. They often have great vision—in the midst of the smoke and fire of overload that disables others, HPPs can see where they need to go and are determined to get there. They have the vision of an eagle and the jaws of a pit bull.

There are three downsides to being an HPP. First, *they often lack good warning signals*. While most of us feel pain when we're pushing at 110 percent of capacity, HPPs often don't notice anything is wrong until they reach 140 percent and hit a wall. Second, *they often set up unrealistic standards for others*. Because God has enabled them to flourish on eighteen-hour days, they often expect the same of others. They don't realize they have an unusual gift; they just think others are weak or lack faith. Third, *they often dole out acceptance based on performance*. It makes sense to pay employees based on performance. But HPPs often think performance is all that matters. They often undervalue things God values highly: love, compassion, justice, faithfulness, purity, prayer, obedience, kindness, and gentleness.

On the other end of the spectrum are Highly Sensitive People (HSP). They are not unproductive, but their strengths are different from those of HPPs. HSPs have antennae for emotional pain and social discord. Even with subtle indicators, they can tell when the social hierarchy is being unkind. They are also particularly susceptible to insults and violence in the media. They need more rest and solitude than other people because their batteries are discharged by all this sensitivity to others. They often are creative. They live in a world in their heads and are good company for themselves on long car rides. They dream a lot. They don't try to control others because they intuitively understand how complicated that process is. They are more susceptible to overload than others because the world's loudspeaker is always on for them. These interesting people make a special contribution to the world, but often at a greater emotional price than others pay.

22. Would you say you are an HPP, an HSP, or somewhere in-between? What makes you say that?

23. Do you have any HPPs in your life whose expectations you feel? If so, who are they, and how do they affect you?

24. Do you have conflict or disappointment regarding someone because he or she isn't as productive as you expect? If so, how (if at all) does this HPP-HSP spectrum bear on that situation?

25. Has it been helpful for you to put your expectations into words on paper? If so, how have you benefited?

26. Take some time to pray about your expectations. Talk with God about each of the expectations you listed in this session. Ask whether it is a reasonable desire or something you are demanding from God. How do your expectations affect your attitude toward God?

The solution for burdensome expectations is contentment. What exactly is contentment, and how does one get it? That will be the topic of session 7.

For Further Study
The Overload Syndrome, chapters 1, 8

For Groups
Share what you learned from this study about your expectations. How reasonable are your expectations? Were you surprised in any areas when you put your expectations into words?

Was the information about HPPs and HSPs helpful? If so, how?

Pray about the expectations you each have for yourselves, as well as those you feel directed at you from other people. Ask God for clarity and the wisdom to know what to do about unreasonable expectations.

Notes
1. John Leo, "Decadence, The Corporate Way," *U.S. News & World Report,* 28 August–4 September 1995, p. 31.
2. Juliet B. Schor, *The Overspent American* (New York: Basic Books, 1998).

"Come, all you who are thirsty,
   come to the waters;
   and you who have no money,
   come, buy and eat!
   Come, buy wine and milk
   without money and without cost.
   Why spend money on what is not bread,
   and your labor on what does not satisfy?
   Listen, listen to me, and eat what is good,
   and your soul will delight in the richest of fare."
   (Isaiah 55:1-2)

Contentment

The antidote to burdensome expectations is contentment. However, contentment is easily misunderstood, and our culture makes true contentment hard to maintain. Your objectives in this session are:

- To understand what biblical contentment is and isn't.
- To evaluate your areas of contentment and discontent.
- To learn some ways of cultivating contentment.

Many people have mistaken notions of what contentment is. It isn't denying one's feelings about unhappiness, but instead is a freedom from being controlled by those feelings. It isn't pretending things are right when they are not, but instead is the peace that comes from knowing God is bigger than any problem and that He works them all out for our good.

Contentment isn't the complacency that defeats any attempt to make things better, but instead is the willingness to work tirelessly for improvement, clinging to God rather than results. It isn't a feeling of well-being contingent on keeping circumstances under control, but instead is a joy that exists in spite of circumstances and looks to the God who never varies. It isn't the comfortable feeling we get when all our needs and desires are met, but instead is the security in knowing, as A. W. Tozer reminds us, that "the man who has God for his treasure has all things in One." [1]

Finally, contentment isn't that pseudovirtue of the "American dream" where we claim solidarity with Paul from the easy chair of middle-class America. We profess to having learned the secret of contentment in all circumstances, yet unlike Paul, we've never experienced forty lashes, stoning, shipwreck, hunger, thirst, homelessness, or imprisonment. Perhaps none of us should presume maturity until the truer tests have been endured. To snuggle up alongside Paul and profess contentment without having known want seems a bit impudent on our part. Paul's contentment in need and plenty is

> I have learned to be content whatever the circumstances. I know what it is to be in need, and I know what it is to have plenty. I have learned the secret of being content in any and every situation, whether well fed or hungry, whether living in plenty or in want.
> (Philippians 4:11-12)

mostly of interest because of the need. Until we know true need and survive the test, we must not presume to be his companion.

1. Think about the above definition of contentment. Which of the following are areas in which you need to grow?

   □ Acknowledging unhappy feelings honestly
   □ Freedom from the control of unhappy feelings
   □ Facing problems squarely
   □ Confidence that God is bigger than my problems
   □ Willingness to work tirelessly to make things better, while trusting God for the results
   □ Joy regardless of circumstances
   □ Ability to maintain faith, hope, and love when the comforts of middle-class life are withdrawn

   Some people have been so deeply disappointed at key moments in life that they fear to dream, to hope, or even to desire. It feels safer to settle for the status quo than to risk longing for their relationships to be richer, their joy deeper, or the suffering of the world addressed. Oddly enough, contentment about material things (such as the size of our house) frees us to be divinely discontented about more important things: how well we know God, how honest and loving our relationships are, and the sufferings of people less fortunate than ourselves.

2. What is one thing you truly hope or long for that has nothing to do with material comfort or success?

3. How easy was it for you to come up with an answer to question 2? Why do you suppose that's the case?

Stop and thank God for something.

4. Which is harder for you: to be content with what you have materially, or to be divinely discontent with the things God is discontented with (such as injustice and sin in the world and in your life)?

Longing for richer relationships is easily subverted into finding fault with people. "If only my wife were more appealing or more sexually interested." "If only my husband made more money or had more hair." The difference between *longing* for something rather than *grumbling* about it is that a longing looks to God for ultimate satisfaction. Longing leads us to care more for the other person; grumbling could lead to caring less.

5. Think of a key relationship in your life. What do you long for from that person? Try to state your longing as a *longing* rather than a *grumbling*.

Discontentment has so many disadvantages one wonders why it is popular. It can suffocate freedom, leaving us in bondage to our desires. It can poison relationships with jealousy and competition. It often rewards blessing with ingratitude toward God. It produces joyless self-pity. The advantages of contentment, on the other hand, include freedom, gratitude, rest, and peace—all components of health. They who are content need not:

- Worry about the latest styles.
- Feel inferior to those who succeed.
- Worry about aging.
- Worry about how to afford this or that.
- Worry about how to get out of debt.

We relate better to God when we are satisfied with what He gives. We relate better to ourselves when we don't constantly berate ourselves for not being smarter, funnier, richer, better looking, taller, thinner, or more athletic. We relate better to others when seeing them doesn't remind us of something they have that we want.

"Expect more and you'll get it," says the MasterCard ad. Implicit in this message is that it is always *appropriate* to expect more. But as we adjust our expectations downward, we will discover less to be unhappy about. If we always expect success and prosperity, we are destined to be chronically frustrated. But if we understand that humankind is fallen and life is difficult, we are more likely to be contented with the simple blessings God sends our way.

Perhaps the best way to deal with the expectation of having enough is to diminish our definition of that word *enough*. If *enough* means "more than we have now," then we will be frustrated. But if *enough* is restricted to needs, then most of us will find that in most areas of life we have enough.

6. How would contentment improve your life?

7. List ten things about your life for which you are grateful.

8. How easy is it for you to feel *genuinely and deeply* grateful for these things? Why do you suppose that's the case?

Money was one of Jesus' favorite topics because it's so deceptive. It seems to meet our short-term needs. It buys food, shelter, vehicles, experiences, a feeling of security, influence over others, and respect from others. However, it doesn't buy our long-term needs: love, truth, relationship, and redemption. Money gives a thrill but no satiety—even the rich find they still want just a little more money.

SOMEONE in the crowd said to him, "Teacher, tell my brother to divide the inheritance with me."

Jesus replied, "Man, who appointed me a judge or an arbiter between you?" Then he said to them, "Watch out! Be on your guard against all kinds of greed; a man's life does not consist in the abundance of his possessions."

And he told them this parable: "The ground of a certain

rich man produced a good crop. He thought to himself, 'What shall I do? I have no place to store my crops.'

"Then he said, 'This is what I'll do. I will tear down my barns and build bigger ones, and there I will store all my grain and my goods. And I'll say to myself, "You have plenty of good things laid up for many years. Take life easy; eat, drink and be merry.'"

"But God said to him, 'You fool! This very night your life will be demanded from you. Then who will get what you have prepared for yourself?'

"This is how it will be with anyone who stores up things for himself but is not rich toward God."

Luke 12:13-21

9. What is the point of Jesus' story about the rich man in Luke 12:13-21?

10. The Bible says greed, envy, and covetousness are sins. What does the world around you think about greed, envy, and covetousness?

11. How does the world's view of greed, envy, and covetousness affect you?

12. Most of us have some dreams about how our lives would be better if we had more money. How would you complete this sentence: "If I were rich, then _____ " ?

Here are a few guidelines for relating to God, people, and things:

1. God comes first and possessions come second (or third, or fourth).
2. Possessions are to be used, not loved.
3. People are to be loved, not used.

13. Do you have any possessions that you treat as though you love them? If so, which ones?

Surely God is good to Israel,
    to those who are pure in heart.
    But as for me, my feet had almost slipped;
    I had nearly lost my foothold.
    For I envied the arrogant
    when I saw the prosperity of the wicked. . . .
    When my heart was grieved
    and my spirit embittered,
    I was senseless and ignorant;
    I was a brute beast before you. . . .
    Whom have I in heaven but you?
    And earth has nothing I desire besides you.
    My flesh and my heart may fail,
    but God is the strength of my heart
    and my portion forever.
    (Psalm 73:1-3,21-22, 25-26)

ALISON will never forget the day she said, "Enough. I have enough." Her children are good enough. In fact, they are remarkable human beings in their own weird ways. Her husband, Paul, is enough, even though she knows all his faults. In fact, since she stopped letting him know every day how much he disappointed her, he has been a lot easier to live with. He watched her warily for the first few weeks when he heard her say things like, "This quirky old house, we have some great memories here, don't we?" Then he seemed to exhale and grow two inches taller.

She set herself the task of writing down ten things she was grateful for every night. At first she could only think of things like, "oxygen." Paul's stubbornness didn't make it to her list for a month. But then one day she realized that "stubbornness" had kept him hanging onto his commitments throughout a difficult period in their marriage and with their kids. After three months, Alison could look around her kitchen, her workplace, or the family room with someone glued to the TV and always find something to be grateful for. The knots in her neck are much looser. Not as loose as she'd like them to be, but loose enough.

14. Why are these possessions so important to you? What do they represent?

15. How would your life be different if you treated God as more important than anything you own or could own?

16. Do you ever put possessions ahead of people? If so, how do you do that?

Paul told the Philippians that contentment is a secret. It will never make sense to the world, and it won't be discovered by science. It's a secret— first you seek it, then it will be revealed to you.

17. What areas of discontent in your life has this session uncovered?

18. For the next week, try raising your awareness of contentment and its enemies. Here are some steps you can take:

Tune out ads. If you're watching television, hit the mute button on your remote when the commercials come on (or better still, turn the TV off). If you're reading a magazine, deliberately skip the ads. Don't read any ads or catalogs that come in the mail.

Listen for discontented thoughts as they arise in your mind. Listen for envy of what others have, or grumbling about what you don't have. Note fantasies about a partner who would be better than your spouse (or your lack of spouse). As they arise, tell them, "You are discontentment. You are envy. You are grumbling against God."

Practice gratitude. As you go through your day, go out of your way to find things to thank God for. Don't stifle longings that are mixed in with that gratitude (you don't have to pretend to yourself that you're happy when you're not, or that things are better than they are). Gratitude can coexist with longing. In fact, telling yourself the truth about your longings, as opposed to your grumbling, may free you to be more grateful in the midst of your situation.

Schedule time for silence. Aim for fifteen minutes of time alone in silence this week. Spend a little time counting your blessings, then just sit and let contentment and peace wash over you. If you find anxiety or preoccupation washing over you instead, try not to get frustrated. Just keep setting those thoughts aside and turn your mind back to God.

In session 8, you'll take a look at another set of forces that may be blocking you from building margin into your life. Threats and promises from various sources work alongside progress and expectations to become powerful motivation for accepting overload. And just as contentment is an antidote to expectations, so faith is an antidote to the fear generated by threats and promises.

For Further Study

Margin, chapter 11

For Groups

Focus your discussion on questions 1, 2, 5, and 7. Read your list in question 7 aloud to the group—how does it feel to do that?

Then select from questions 9-16 a question or two that gets at what you learned about yourself and possessions. Spend particular time on question 17. Then talk about what you learned from the exercise in question 18.

Use your prayer time primarily for thanksgiving.

Notes

1. A.W. Tozer, *The Pursuit of God* (Harrisburg, PA: Christian Publications, 1948), p. 20.

Threats and Promises

We have begun to zero in on the beliefs, values, and emotions that make it seem that reducing our load in any given area is not an option. We've looked at the pressure of progress, the success ethic, and expectations.

In session 1 we confronted the fact that we have limits. For some of us, facing our limits is frightening. It might mean we don't have what it takes to get what we need to survive. For others, accepting limits seems like a lack of faith. Doesn't God call us to do greater things than we can imagine? It turns out, however, that coming to grips with our limits is one of the most faith-filled steps we can take. It requires confronting our fears, as well as the ways in which our culture pressures us to accept overload.

Your objectives in this session are:

- To understand how our culture rewards overload and punishes margin.
- To explore how fear might keep you locked in overload.
- To struggle with God over fear versus faith.

1. Look back at what you wrote in question 7 of session 1. Look also at the expectations you listed in session 6. Take a few minutes to think again about the messages you get from work, church, friends, family, and the media about working, volunteering, spending, achieving, watching, listening, and doing more.

    What *threats* do these people and institutions make? (For instance, "If you don't work this weekend, then _____." "If you don't participate in this church activity, then _____." "If you don't buy this product, then _____.")

"Do not be afraid of those who kill the body but cannot kill the soul. Rather, be afraid of the One who can destroy both soul and body in hell. Are not two sparrows sold for a penny? Yet not one of them will fall to the ground apart from the will of your Father. And even the very hairs of your head are all numbered. So don't be afraid; you are worth more than many sparrows."

(Matthew 10:28-31)

2. What promises do these people and organizations make? ("If you go all out for this, then _____." "If you buy this, then _____.")

3. Assign the following items to one of four categories in the chart on the next page according to their importance to you. Try to order these items according to the way you *do* value them, not according to how you think you *should* value them.

    career success
    a higher economic standard of living ten years from now
    rest
    stimulating leisure activities
    power
    people's respect
    influence
    strong intimate relationships with people
    competing and winning
    a deep relationship with God
    expression of my creativity
    excitement
    tranquility
    helping others and/or society
    change and variety
    stability
    knowledge
    security

among my highest values	a secondary value	desirable but not very important	unimportant or undesirable

Again, the devil took [Jesus] to a very high mountain and showed him all the kingdoms of the world and their splendor. "All this I will give you," he said, "if you will bow down and worship me."

Jesus said to him, "Away from me, Satan! For it is written: 'Worship the Lord your God, and serve him only.'"
(Matthew 4:8-10)

4. a. Take a minute to think of what you most want right now. Write down that thing or those things.

   b. Now, think about what having those things would give you. What do you want even more than those things offer?

   c. Now, think about what you wrote for (b). What do you want even more than (b) offers you?

   d. Now think about (c). What do you really, really want that you would have if you had (c)?

JACOB is beginning to realize how many of his choices are driven by a promise that hangs just beyond his reach: his mother's voice whispering, "If you made as much money as Mark, then I'd really love you."

   Russell is recognizing an implicit threat that drives him: "If you don't keep performing, you're not a real man."

   Candice has discovered how deeply she believes her life

depends on making everyone happy: her children, her husband, the people at church, her family and friends. She imagines them threatening, "If you say no to us, then we won't like you." But are they all really saying that, or is she imagining it? And if she did say no, and someone didn't like her, would that be the end of her life?

Jacob longs to be loved, securely and without manipulation. Russell wants to be respected, even admired. Candice wants to feel connected to people who value her. All three of them want their lives to have meaning, to be about something, not just to rush headlong from meaningless activity to activity, driven by hopes and fears. They think they'd settle for happiness, but what they really long for is joy.

> "The kingdom of heaven is like treasure hidden in a field. When a man found it, he hid it again, and then in his joy went and sold all he had and bought that field."
> (Matthew 13:44)

By now you're probably getting down to some deep longings, like love that will never fail you, or joy, or a sense that your life matters.

Compare the threats and promises you named in questions 1 and 2 to the values and longings you expressed in questions 3 and 4. Chances are that if you are letting yourself be severely overloaded in some area, it's because you *believe* that this overload offers you something you deeply long for, and you *fear* that cutting back in this area may cost you something you deeply value. The threats and promises work because they touch on your deep desires and fears.

5. For example, how does overloading yourself at work promise to meet each of these deep desires?

the admiration and respect of other people

a sense that your life matters

security of food, water, clothing, and shelter

6. The number one reason women say they buy a cell phone is for physical security in case their car breaks down. Cell phones address women's deep fear of physical attack. What other fears or desires might drive people's decision to be accessible at all times by phone, fax, and/or modem?

7. What fears or desires might be behind information overload behaviors, such as keeping stacks of unread magazines and journals, extensive Web browsing, and anxiety over information?

8. What fears or deep desires might motivate a person to volunteer excessive amounts of time at church?

9. What fears or deep desires might move a person to go into debt in order to accumulate material possessions?

10. How would you complete the following sentences? (Omit any that you think don't apply to you.)

    I fear that if I lived within limits, then . . .

I push beyond my limits because I believe I need . . .

I push beyond my limits because I want . . .

I push beyond my limits because I believe I should be . . .

I push beyond my limits because I value . . .

The antidote to fear is faith. If we believe in our heart of hearts that God is a good and powerful God who will provide what we need and who cares about what we deeply long for, then we don't have to fear what might happen if we reduced our load. If we believe that God is able to build His kingdom even if we get a good night's sleep and we say "no" to certain worthwhile activities, then we can accept the limited but important role we have in building the kingdom.

11. Read Luke 12:22-34 below. According to Jesus . . .

- What is very important in life?

- What is less important?

- Why should we not worry or be afraid about getting our needs met?

THEN Jesus said to his disciples: "Therefore I tell you, do not worry about your life, what you will eat; or about your body, what you will wear. Life is more than food, and the body more than clothes. Consider the ravens: They do not sow or reap, they have no storeroom or barn; yet God feeds them. And how much more valuable you are than birds! Who of you by worrying can add a single hour to his life? Since you cannot do this very little thing, why do you worry about the rest?

"Consider how the lilies grow. They do not labor or spin. Yet I tell you, not even Solomon in all his splendor was dressed like one of these. If that is how God clothes the grass of the field, which is here today, and tomorrow is thrown into the fire, how much more will he clothe you, O you of little faith! And do not set your heart on what you will eat or drink; do not worry about it. For the pagan world runs after all such things, and your Father knows that you need them. But seek his kingdom, and these things will be given to you as well.

"Do not be afraid, little flock, for your Father has been pleased to give you the kingdom. Sell your possessions and give to the poor. Provide purses for yourselves that will not wear out, a treasure in heaven that will not be exhausted, where no thief comes near and no moth destroys. For where your treasure is, there your heart will be also."

(Luke 12:22-34)

12. Play devil's advocate for a moment. Give your best argument for not relying on what Jesus says here.

13. How do you think Jesus would respond to your argument?

14. What, for you, are the primary obstacles to deep faith?

15. Pray about seeking God's kingdom ahead of the things the world runs after. What might that look like in your life? What risks are involved? Are the risks worth it? Talk to God about your thoughts on this.

For Groups

Compare notes on your answers to questions 1-4. What do you learn about each other's fears and longings? In what ways are your fears and longings similar? What differences do you observe? Certain deep fears and longings are common to all humans, while others vary according to our personalities and culture.

Review your answers to questions 5-9. What insights are helpful or significant to you? Share those with the group.

Share your answers to questions 10 and 14.

Discuss questions 12 and 13. Feel free to set up a debate between Jesus and the world or the Devil. Give Jesus your best arguments, then give some real thought to how He would respond.

Close by confessing your fears to God and asking God to strengthen your faith.

The Primacy of Love

Some people think seeking God's kingdom requires an all-out effort of eighteen-hour days. To them, deep faith means believing that by faith they can do far more than they could ask or imagine—and by "doing far more" they mean spending more hours at more intensity than their bodies were designed to handle. The trouble is that no matter how hard we work, there is always more work to do in building God's kingdom. There are always more people to serve, more people who haven't heard the gospel, and more need for justice and righteousness in the world.

But is seeking God's kingdom a matter of *productivity* or *process*? Is building the kingdom a matter of numbers (over a billion people served) or depth? How productive or efficient is prayer? How productive or efficient is love?

In this session you will look at productivity and love. Your objectives in this session are:

- To think about what love is.
- To examine how love currently fits into your system of priorities.
- To decide how you want love to fit into your system of priorities.

God does not give out monthly productivity sheets. All He asks is, "Do you love Me?" Such love is not measured by units per hour (productivity), but rather by consistently loving the person standing in front of you at the moment (process). It does not have to do with the past nor the future, but the present—right now. Are you bringing the kingdom of God to bear on whatever you are doing—right now?

Let's take the world of medical practice as an example. A productivity model would say that if I see thirty patients a day rather than twenty, I am a better doctor. Rewards will follow. Does this mean that seeing fifty patients is better than thirty? Or seeing one hundred patients is better than fifty? Obviously, as productivity is pushed to extremes, process begins to suffer. I can tell you from experience that an over-emphasis on medical productivity displaces caring, compassion, and service.

God does not have to depend on human exhaustion to get His work done. Chronic overloading is not a spiritual prerequisite for authentic Christianity. Quite the contrary: overloading is often what we do when we forget who God is.

Our contemporary drivenness assumes that God never reaches down and says, "Enough, my child. Well done. Now go home and love your children. Encourage your spouse. Rest. Pray. Meditate. Sleep. Recharge your batteries. I'll have more for you to do tomorrow. And, by the way, don't worry. Remember who you are dealing with."

Whoever does not love does not know God, because God is love.
(1 John 4:8)

1. How many of the past twenty-four hours have you devoted to productivity?

"Teacher, which is the greatest commandment in the Law?"
Jesus replied: "'Love the Lord your God with all your heart and with all your soul and with all your mind.' This is the first and greatest command-ment. And the second is like it: 'Love your neigh-bor as yourself.'"
(Matthew 22:36-39)

2. How many of the past twenty-four hours have you devoted to love (caring, listening, building a relationship, serving people's practical needs)?

3. For those in ministry or helping professions, it can be especially hard to tell when we are treating people as units that need to be served productively and when we are treating them as persons who need to be loved. Think of times when you have visited a doctor, minister, counselor, advisor, or other helper. What actions on their part make you feel like either a production unit or a person?

> The entire law is summed up in a single command: "Love your neighbor as yourself."
> (Galatians 5:14)

4. Do you really believe that God wants your love more than your productivity? What helps you or blocks you from believing this?

> If I have the gift of prophecy and can fathom all mysteries and all knowledge, and if I have a faith that can move mountains, but have not love, I am nothing.
> (1 Corinthians 13:2)

There are many reasons to reduce overload. For instance, it can save our lives. But the most important reason is that God created us for love. There's no theological debate about it—love is the goal of the Christian life.

5. Read the Scripture passages on this and the facing page. What evidence do we have that love is the goal of the Christian life?

On that day when everything is forced through the fire of judgment, love is the only thing that will exit out the other side. It will stand alone, vindicated. It will finally and clearly be seen for the dominant, unbeatable, infinite, glorified force it has always been, just obscured for millennia by layers of fallen clutter. We were put here to love and serve people every day of our lives. Success is nothing more than that. Anyone who says that success is more than that is not basing it on truth.

Yet overload wars against love. We try to focus on our spouse, a child, or a friend but find that a dozen activities intervene. Soon the spouse leaves for a meeting, the child goes to soccer practice, and the friend goes to a class across town. These activities have merit, but in profusion they dilute our focus. Relationship is replaced by experience, and even experience is watered down.

Distraction also disrupts love. Interruptions are so much a part of daily living that we often don't recognize them as pathogens. When an issue is important, we need to live with it, dwell on it, lock on it. It may take days, years, or a lifetime. Love, like all aspects of spiritual maturity, takes that kind of time and focus. Perhaps we need to focus on parenting but are distracted by a new car that requires more debt and more work. Perhaps we need to cultivate the habit of humility by saying, "I'm sorry," but just when we have gotten ourselves together to speak, our pager goes off.

6. Until now, how has your definition of success differed from a definition based in love?

7. How do activities hinder your ability to focus on loving the people in your life?

8. How do distractions and interruptions hinder your focus on caring for people?

"It's become clearer and clearer to me that if families just let this culture happen to them, they end up fat, addicted, broke, with a house full of junk and no time." [1]

9. How does the drive for productivity hinder you from loving?

IT has been a shock for Dave and Candice to realize that letting their own relationship slide has not been an expression of love for either their children or their church. They have decided to withdraw from volunteering for a year so they can get to know each other again. They have also asked each of their children to choose one extracurricular activity this year so their schedules will not be so frantic.

Jacob balked at first when he realized he needed to make loving others more of a priority than doing whatever it would take to earn his mother's approval. But having begun to take steps in that direction, he's a lot more relaxed. Instead of constantly asking him-self the futile question, "What can I do to be as successful as Mark?" he's now practicing every day asking the question, "How can I express love for someone today?" That's something he can actually succeed at.

Russell loves risk, so when he saw that betting his life on love rather than career was going to be the biggest rush of his life, he started really getting into it. The hard part is that many people around him don't see love as the measure of a real man, so Russell has joined a men's group where the other men remind him that he's made the right choice.

10. Think about your day tomorrow. A hundred years from now, what will you wish you had done with that day?

Jesus calls us to love on several levels. First, we are to love those closest to us: family members and those people who support us in the life of faith. Second, we are to love our neighbors—that is, anyone in need, whether they live next door or on the other side of the world (Luke 10:25-37). Third, we are to love our enemies (Luke 6:27-36). That's a tall order. Obviously, it's impossible to give significant time and attention to every person on the planet. To prevent relationship overload, we could start by focusing on our immediate family and closest friends, a few people in need, and one person with whom we are in conflict. We might exercise our love muscles by paying attention to the people who cross our path each day: the cashier at the grocery store, the person who takes our money at the parking garage, the dentist's receptionist.

In fact, far from requiring us to stretch ourselves to the relational breaking point, love actually demands margin. Jesus' instructions to walk the second mile, carry others' burdens, witness to the Truth at every opportunity, and teach our children when we sit, walk, lie, and stand all presuppose we have margin and we make it available for His purposes. *Obedience to these commands is often not schedulable.*

Margin is not a spiritual necessity. But availability is. God expects us to be available for others' needs. But without margin, we have great difficulty guaranteeing availability. When God calls, He gets a busy signal.

11. What might it cost you to invest time and energy in loving people? What risks are involved?

He has shown you, O man, what is good.
    And what does the LORD require of you?
    To act justly and to love mercy
    and to walk humbly with your God.
    (Micah 6:8)

12. Someone might argue, "Earning money is the way I give love to my family. That's how I meet their genuine, legitimate needs. And it takes everything I've got." How would you respond to that? (For instance, what does a family need besides money? Is there a way for you to provide for your family's material needs and still have something left over for their other needs?)

Love costs, but love is also good for us. A strong support system is the most important protection against the debilitating effects of stress. Relentlessly serving others can be like running up the stairs of the Washington Monument—it can lead to a heart attack—but consistently serving others within our limits is like aerobic exercise—it strengthens our hearts.

13. How could treating love as a priority improve your life? What benefits do you foresee?

In sessions 11 and 12, you will make an action plan to build margin into your life. You'll consider suggestions for addressing activity, work, debt, access, information, and other overloads. You will want this plan to be realistic and suited to your personality and life situation. The specifics of your plan are a matter of your preference, but your goals need to be guided by God's value system. At the top of God's agenda for you is not that your life work with minimum pain. The top of God's agenda is that you create enough margin to love God and people well over the long haul and within your realistic limits.

14. Make a list of the people with whom you want to begin your focus on love. Make a reasonable list on which you can focus during the next six months while you are beginning to make changes in your life. Include family/friends, at least one or two "neighbors," and at least one "enemy."

> If anyone has material possessions and sees his brother in need but has no pity on him, how can the love of God be in him?
> (1 John 3:17)

For Further Study
The Overload Syndrome, Conclusion

For Groups
Talk about what love means in your real-life situations. What time, emotional energy, engagement, forgiveness, listening, and kindness does loving the people in your life require? How do you manage that? How does love conflict with the expectations for productivity and success that you also feel?

Pray for the people whom you want to love well over the long haul. Pray also for one another.

Notes
1. Mary Pipher in *Family Therapy Networker*, "The Day We Live In," *Current Thoughts and Trends*, July 1997, p. 14.

Balance and Priorities

Much is made today of the virtues of excellence. But what does this mean? Often the excellence described is only in one narrow corridor of life: virtuosos who exist only for their music or corporate executives who live at the office.

What do these passionate high-achievers think of balance? For many, it is an enemy. Single-minded fervency is their standard. One-hundred-percent effort is the minimum, and those who question such asymmetrical dedication are distrusted and unpromoted.

In this session you will perform a critical comparison of the concepts of balance, excellence, and priorities. Your objectives are:

- To understand what balance and excellence involve.
- To assess the pros and cons of each.
- To decide whether you will choose balance or excellence as a guide for your priorities.

While undivided devotion to one cause can bring great success and vault a person into prominence, such a priority structure often leaves the rest of that person's life in a state of disorder. Thus it is not uncommon to discover a physician who fails as a parent, an entertainer who fails as a spouse, a pastor who neglects personal health, or an executive who fails at all three. Traditional wisdom has told us not to put all our eggs in one basket. Yet, in pursuit of single-minded excellence, we often discard this basic wisdom. Balance is not the goal; preeminence is the goal.

I am not advocating halfheartedness and mediocrity, for we always ought to do our best. But doing our best has limits. Our rush toward excellence in one quadrant of life must not be permitted to cause destruction in another. "We need," as Norman Cousins explains, "to be more proportionate." Some aspects of excellence are appropriate and desirable. At other times, however, the pursuit of ultraexcellence can lead to a dangerous imbalance and dysfunction.

Those who go all out for success in one endeavor, points out physicist/engineer Richard H. Bube, risk failure in other important areas of life. "Not only is the ability to exhibit excellence in other fields decreased, but in several fields the net consequence is to produce what we may colloquially call 'negative excellence.'" Bube recommends "a more balanced approach." [1] This principle is demonstrated in figures 10.1 and 10.2 (adapted from Bube).

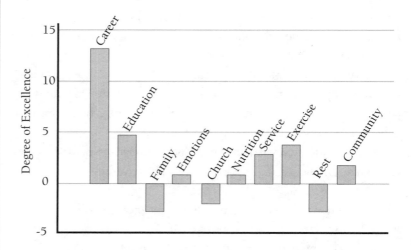

Figure 10.1: Excellence Plus Failure

Godliness with contentment is great gain. For we brought nothing into the world, and we can take nothing out of it. But if we have food and clothing, we will be content with that. People who want to get rich fall into temptation and a trap and into many foolish and harmful desires that plunge men into ruin and destruction. For the love of money is a root of all kinds of evil. Some people, eager for money, have wandered from the faith and pierced themselves with many griefs. (1 Timothy 6:6-10)

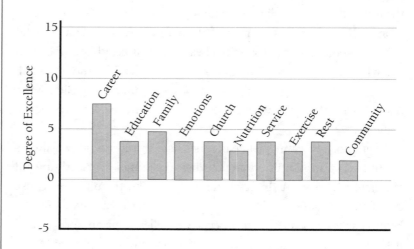

Figure 10.2: Balance

The person in figure 10.1 has chosen to strive for such a high degree of excellence in one area that other areas reveal little excellence or even "negative excellence" (that is, failure). Consequently, this person has achieved excellence in his or her career but, at the same time, has suffered failure in the other important areas of family, church, and rest.

In contrast, the person in figure 10.2 has chosen to live a balanced life and has therefore avoided "negative excellence" in any area. As a consequence, no outstanding level of excellence has been achieved. On the other hand, no failure has been experienced either.

If you wish to achieve excellence but also to have life balance, beware. Those who advocate excellence at all costs often do not believe in "outside interests" and may not tolerate them. Family, friends, church, as well as margin in personal time and emotional health—all are luxuries that may compete with a stellar performance in a single area. If, then, we are forced to choose between excellence and balance, how do we choose? Once we understand that God expects us to act responsibly in each area of life, it is easier to discern the problems associated with one-track excellence.

1. How important has the pursuit of excellence been to you in your life so far?

2. When is excellence right and appropriate? When is it wrong and inappropriate?

3. What is the difference between wanting excellence and wanting perfection?

Saying *no* is not an excuse for noninvolvement, laziness, or insensitivity. Instead, it is purely a mechanism for living by our priorities, allowing God to direct our lives rather than the world, and preserving our vitality for the things that really matter.

4. In what areas (if any) have you tried to excel?

5. What have been the results, both positive and negative?

   positive

   negative

6. When you think about giving up a measure of excellence in *one* area of your life in order to have some measure of success in *all* areas, what does that feel like? (Frustrating? Scary? Impossible? Okay? A relief?)

If we accept that balance is important, especially in light of avoiding "negative excellence" in any area of life, how do we achieve it? Since each of us lives according to a set of priorities—whether we are aware of it or not—perhaps that is the place to start.

What does your priority list look like? For those committed to ultra-excellence, one goal stands alone on the top—perhaps wealth, power, athletic success, academics, or political victory. Sequentially beneath this exalted goal are myriad subordinate goals. These form a constellation of priorities for each person. If written down, one list might look something like this:

1. God
2. Spouse/marriage
3. Children
4. Self
5. Work
6. Church
7. Friends, neighbors
8. Health
9. Security
10. Civic duty

Does creating such lists help us solve our problem and lead us to biblically authentic decision making? I think not. "A list of priorities doesn't make sense!" observes J. Grant Howard in *Balancing Life's Demands*. "No matter how you define and describe your particular approach, if it is a sequential approach, it is loaded with contradictions." [2]

We cannot achieve balance by stacking our priorities one on top of another, even though this is a common practice. As Dr. Howard goes on to advise, it fits better to think of God as *central* to everything and then build outward from that point. We do not love God, *then* spouse, *then* children, *then* self, *then* church. We love God, spouse, children, self, and church all at the same time. Similarly, we do not love God 100 percent, spouse 95 percent, children 90 percent, church 80 percent. God's standard requires that we love all of them all of the time.

One of the interesting things about love is that it is not a mathematical entity. When divided, love multiplies. However we attempt to factor it, love remains an intact whole. For example, if we have one child in our family, we might be singularly devoted to that child and love him or her 100 percent. If we have a second child, does that mean we love each child only 50 percent? Of course not. We would love each child 100 percent even if there were ten of them. God has suspended the laws of mathematics in allowing love to expand infinitely. In so doing, He has delivered us from the need to prioritize our love sequentially.

It does not make sense to have sequential priorities in terms of love or even in terms of commitment. We love each person fully. Additionally, we are committed to doing good in all areas of life. Priority thinking *is* appropriate when we speak of time, however.

It is unwise to give all our time to work and family, but none to personal health. God created us to need health, and it is not wrong to seek it. Likewise, God created us to need each other in relationship. It is not wrong to dedicate time for that. He created us with duties toward nature, work, and government, and it is not wrong for us to focus on these duties. *But the time devoted must be balanced, for if we give too much in one area we neglect our duty in another important area and fail God's requirements for balanced living.*

Partitioning our time is probably the most important practical issue in achieving balanced living. Yet rationing it wisely presents a dilemma for each of us. In attempting to live a full life, we taste every experience. In attempting to be good parents, we try to give our children more opportunities than we had. In attempting to be compassionate, we want to help with everyone's problems. In attempting to be good providers, we accept extra work assignments.

7. How is your time partitioned? What factors influence—or even dictate—how you apportion your time?

8. In some areas of life God requires a "decent minimum"—a standard below which you will fail God's standard and experience pain or dysfunction. In what areas of life does God require that we give a "decent minimum"? List all such areas below.

9. With regard to the list just completed, how much time do you think represents such a "decent minimum" per week?

10. In what areas of your life will you need to cut back your time commitment in order to achieve more balance?

11. What are the potential costs of giving up single-minded excellence as a goal?

What are you hurrying
toward?

12. What are the potential benefits?

13. What is it about our society that makes pursuing excellence in certain areas (at the expense of relationships or health, if necessary) seem so important?

14. If you gave up the goal of excellence, at all costs, in your career (and the applause that goes with it), what would make you feel valuable as a person?

15. Other than the pursuit of excellence, what factors in your life war against balance?

16. What is the "one thing" Jesus is referring to in Luke 10? What practical implications would it have for our lives if we placed this "one thing" central to everything else?

17. On your death bed, how will you wish your priorities had been structured? One million years from now (in eternity), how will you wish your priorities had been structured? Any changes from your current priority structure?

As Jesus and his disciples were on their way, he came to a village where a woman named Martha opened her home to him. She had a sister called Mary, who sat at the Lord's feet listening to what he said. But Martha was distracted by all the preparations that had to be made. She came to him and asked, "Lord, don't you care that my sister has left me to do the work by myself? Tell her to help me!"

"Martha, Martha," the Lord answered, "you are worried and upset about many things, but only one thing is needed. Mary has chosen what is better, and it will not be taken away from her."

(Luke 10:38-42)

Pray about excellence versus balance. Talk to God about the costs and benefits of each way of structuring your life. Tell God how you're feeling about the tradeoff and what you want to do. Ask God to show you what your life would look like with Him at the center.

For Groups

Discuss excellence versus balance. Which (if either) have you been pursuing recently? What have been the results? Which do you want to pursue in the next five years? How will that look, in practical terms? What has led you to that decision? What might be the costs of that decision? How do you feel about that?

Offer each other constructive feedback about the priorities each of you has expressed. Do they seem godly? Realistic?

In sessions 11 and 12 you will form a concrete action plan for the next six months that attempts to put your priorities into practice. As you close, pray for each other about this important endeavor.

Notes

1. Richard H. Bube, "On the Pursuit of Excellence: Pitfalls in the Effort to Become No. 1," *Perspectives on Science and Christian Faith,* June 1987, pp. 70-71. Used by permission.
2. J. Grant Howard, *Balancing Life's Demands: A New Perspective on Priorities* (Portland, OR: Multnomah, 1983), p. 37.

Taking Action I

Having looked at reasons why you're overloaded and the sound spiritual and health reasons for restoring margin to your life, you're ready to plan a course of action. There is an enormous number of steps you could take, and for each one you may have six reasons why you can't take it. Chances are that you may have to trade some productivity (and therefore money, praise, career advancement, status, possessions) for rest, relationships, and spiritual maturity. This may be a scary tradeoff, so be aware of your inner reactions as you read through the suggestions in this session and session 12.

Don't feel you must cover sessions 11 and 12 in two weeks. (It makes no sense to overload yourself with a plan to reduce your overload!) Take as long as you need to make a realistic plan. It may be most effective for you to make slow but consistent headway in restructuring the next six months of your life. You will address a total of twelve life areas in your action plan; if you're really overloaded and can't handle any more rapid change, you could deal with just one area per week for twelve weeks. In three months, you'll have made great progress at a gradual pace.

In this session you will make an action plan for six areas of your life: accessibility, information, media, activity, hurry, and emotions. Your objectives in this session are:

- To find steps you can take that will create margin in your life.
- To consider both the costs and benefits of taking these steps.
- To evaluate this plan according to two criteria: Is it realistic? (That is, do the benefits outweigh the costs? Is it within my limits?) And, will it help me love better?

In the next few pages are ideas for action in the six areas listed above. You may want to read them through once and check the box beside each one that you think would be helpful for you. Then you can go back through the list with your calendar handy. Identify those action steps on which you intend to follow through in the next six months. If you identify only three items in each category, that's a start. You can prioritize your action steps on pages 148-153. For each step, decide whether it is something you want to do this week, this month, next month, consistently for the next six months, or sometime in the next six months. Write action steps in your calendar as appropriate.

On the other hand, perhaps you like one of the ideas listed below, but you think there's no way you have the time, freedom, or ability to do it. List any such ideas on page 153 : "Action Steps I'd Take If I Could." You may find that six months from now you have room in your life to take on some of these. Or, you may find that if you do one, that frees you up to do another. For example, most people have to get their spending under control before they can reasonably think about cutting back at work.

Do not approach this action plan as one more thing you are under pressure to achieve! If you have identified the things that drive your tendency to overload, watch that they don't drive your process of change.

Before anything else, take a moment to pray. God made you limited and dependent on Him. God made you with the need for margin. Within the ways of God there is a way for you to fulfill your most important commitments without living in constant overload. Ask God for the insight and courage to make wise and creative plans for changing your life.

Accessibility

1. Look back at your answers to questions 1-3 in session 3. Below are some suggestions for reducing your accessibility overload. (They are explained more fully in chapter 3 of *The Overload Syndrome.*) Check any that you want to put into practice. Then add any other ideas you have.

    ☐ **Decide not to answer your telephone** or pager for _____ hours in the evening when you are sharing a meal and time with your family.

□ **Turn off or unplug the phone** between the hours of _____ and _____. Let an answering machine take messages. Tell your friends and associates you will be unavailable during those hours.

□ **After a business trip, take a day at home** when you don't answer the phone, e-mail, or even the doorbell.

□ **Go to a library or other isolated** place where you can work without interruptions. Turn off your cell phone and ignore your pager.

□ **Plan time late at night or early in the morning** when you can have some uninterrupted time to yourself. (You will have to eliminate something else in order to get enough sleep.)

□ **Use Caller ID.**

□ If you find it overwhelming to come home to full voice mail, **turn it off.** People will call back.

□ **Always refuse telephone solicitations.**

□ **Have your name removed** from direct mail, telemarketing, and e-mail marketing lists. Write to:

(Telemarketing)
Direct Marketing Association
Telephone Preference Service
P.O. Box 9014
Farmingdale, NY 11735

(Direct-mail list)
Direct Marketing Association
Mail Preference Service
P.O. Box 9008
Farmingdale, NY 11735

(e-mail)
Send an e-mail to: remove@cyberpromo.com. Write "Remove all" in the subject or message field. This will remove you from all lists controlled by Cyber Promotions.

□ **Retreat to a local motel** for one or two nights each quarter. (This is really fun for kids if you can afford to take them.) If

Take a slow, deep breath. Exhale slowly.

Stop and thank God for
something.

you want to commit to doing this, write "quarterly retreat" on page 152 ("Action Steps to Take Sometime in the Next Six Months"). On page 148 ("Action Steps to Take This Week") write, "Schedule quarterly retreats for this quarter and next quarter."

□ **Schedule two hours of uninterrupted solitude** twice a month. Spend the time building a relationship with God and yourself.

If you checked this box, write on page 151 ("Action Steps to Take Consistently for the Next Six Months"), "two hours of solitude twice a month." Now look at your calendar. When can you schedule solitude for next week? If next week is already packed, turn to the following week. Even if that week is packed, don't put off solitude. What can you cross out? Television should be the first item to go. If you work more than fifty hours per week, would your business cease to run if you took two hours away?

Here is where your exploration of excellence, balance, and priorities hits the real world. What do you think you might have to sacrifice if you commit to two hours of solitude twice a month? Your job? A promotion? Your family? Four hours alone per month seems like an impossible goal for many people. Yet the dividends of solitude are enormous. Consider making this commitment for the next two months. If you're having trouble actually finding room on your calendar, take a few minutes and describe your conflicts here:

☐ **Schedule a day alone with yourself and God** twice a year. Mark your calendar now.

☐ Other ideas:

Information and Education

2. Look back at your answers to questions 14-17 in session 3. Below are some suggestions for reducing your information overload. (They are explained more fully in chapter 10 of *The Overload Syndrome*.) Check any that you want to put into practice. Then add any other ideas you have.

☐ **Give yourself permission not to know everything.** Practice saying, "I don't know," when someone asks you a question to which you don't know the answer.

☐ **Make a priority of books that have stood the test of time.** Put the Bible, the saints, the classics, and the best of literature ahead of newsmagazines, best sellers, and the Web. Step up a level or two from data to information to knowledge to wisdom.

If you checked the above item, make a plan now to change your reading priorities. List at least three things you're going to do. For instance, "For the next month, I will throw away all newsmagazines as soon as they arrive. On Sunday, I will ask _____ (someone whose wisdom I respect) what books have most affected his or her life. I will write down the titles. I will buy at least one of these books." Write your plan here:

☐ If you tend to overemphasize head learning, **dedicate the next six months to heart training.** One step you could take would be to read one psalm a day. There are 150 of them, so even if you miss thirty days you can get through them in six months. As you read, ask yourself these questions: What does the psalmist believe about God? What emotions does the psalmist express toward God? Toward people? When have I experienced these emotions? How do I deal with emotions like these?

If you checked the above item, write your plan for heart training here:

☐ Make a pile of all the unread periodicals (magazines, newspapers, and journals) you have in your home. (Make a second pile at your office, or combine the two.) If the stack is more than six inches high, save the top inch and throw the rest away. If it is more than two feet high, throw away the whole stack and start fresh.

☐ Go through the list of all the periodicals to which you subscribe. Cancel subscriptions to all but those you really value. Try to trim them down to six or fewer per month unless you have a scheduled time to read periodicals. (Estimate the time per month you have for reading them, and use that as a gauge to know how many to keep.)

The ones I will keep are: _____

_____

_____

_____

Blessed is the man who
finds wisdom,
    the man who gains
understanding,
    for she is more prof-
itable than silver
    and yields better
returns than gold.
    (Proverbs 3:13-14)

□ Regarding paper on your desk: OHIO—**Only Handle It Once.** Use it and then immediately file it or throw it away.

□ **Don't pile assorted paper on your desk,** through which you have to shuffle every time you need to find something. Use separate storage bins or trays for different projects, or start a filing system that works for you.

□ **Clear your desk,** throwing away anything you can and filing the rest.

□ Other ideas:

Media

3. Look back at your answers to question 3 in session 4. Below are some suggestions for reducing your media overload. (They are explained more fully in chapter 11 of *The Overload Syndrome*.) Check any that you want to put into practice. Then add any other ideas you have.

☐ **Make a list** of five things you can do when you are lonely or bored that don't involve television, radio, a movie, or a computer. For instance:

■ List some friends you can call:

_____

_____

_____

■ Invite someone over.
■ Make a coffee date.
■ Visit someone who would welcome the contact.
■ Send an encouraging note to a friend.
■ Your ideas:

☐ **Ban media on a Saturday afternoon** so that your kids are forced to play. Play encourages creativity.

☐ The next time you are planning entertainment, decide to **create it rather than consume it.** Play a sport rather than watch it. Make music rather than just listen to it. Visit someone. Bake. Travel. Have a real experience instead of a virtual one.

Love is not like other resources. There is an infinite supply. In fact, the more it is used, the more its supply increases.

With money, the more you hoard, the richer you become. But with love, the more you spend, the richer you become.

☐ **Limit television in your home.** Here are some possible guidelines (not laws):

___ **Allow up to seven hours of TV (including videos) each week.**

___ Require all viewing to be **preplanned or intentional.**

___ No TV is allowed before homework or chores are done.

___ **One hour per day** can be viewed—and only approved shows.

Exception: two hours for an approved movie.

☐ **Limit the number of TV channels** you receive. Ask your cable carrier to **selectively discontinue MTV** at your home. (They can discontinue one channel; you don't have to take the whole package.) Consider doing this with HBO or other movie channels too.

☐ **Limit the number of TVs in your house** to _____. Consider getting rid of bedroom TVs so you can keep track of what and when your kids are watching.

☐ **Limit hours per week** of Nintendo, Sega, Walkman, and Internet use.

☐ **Have nonelectronic children's birthday parties.** No videos or video games. Create fun activities without media.

☐ **Mute the TV when the commercials begin,** or change channels.

☐ **Have a TV fast**—no TV for a week or month.

☐ **Fast from news for a week.** (See how little you miss.)

☐ **Fast from car radio or CD** for a week. Pray instead, or just enjoy the silence.

Fifty-eight percent of children have a television in their own room.

☐ **Fast from the Internet** for a week.

☐ If you can't bring yourself to fast from a given type of media, you may be addicted. Consider that possibility, and **ask for help from a spiritually mature person.**

☐ **Set aside four nights during the next month to watch TV** or movies with your kids. Let them choose the shows so you can find out what their favorites are. Ask what they like about the shows they choose. (Don't lecture; just listen for their views and values. Next month you can start expressing opinions if you can do so without preaching.) On page 148 ("Action Steps to Take This Week") write, "Schedule four TV nights with kids."

For some reason, evil is always more interesting than virtue. It is hard to create a really interesting TV show—including the news—about virtue. That's why you hear and see so much evil in the media. Media moguls don't love evil more than most people. Some of them don't even let their kids watch what they produce. They are in it for the money; evil sells, and good doesn't. So,

☐ **Practice hating evil.** When you see it, label it as such, if only in your head. Remind yourself not to laugh when someone is dismembered on screen.

☐ **Play soothing music at home.** It may annoy your kids at first, but it's worth a try. Go for quality—if they have to be annoyed, let them be annoyed by something with musical depth.

☐ **Schedule a family video night.** Find a date your whole family can be together sometime in the next two months. Rent a video. (Two movie guides you might find helpful are *Preview* [phone 972-231-9910] and *MovieGuide* [phone 800-899-6684].

☐ **Read aloud to your kids before they go to bed.** Ask your local librarian to recommend appropriate books.

□ **Pay your kids to read.** Try a penny a page—perhaps even a nickel a page. Instead of buying them outdoor or electronic equipment, let them read for it.

□ **Schedule a family reading night.** You can go through the same book, or each person can read his or her own book. Plan snacks, and turn off the phone.

□ Other ideas:

Activity and Commitment

4. **Make a list of all the nonwork activities** you have scheduled for the next month *that you wish you could get out of but can't.*

5. **Think about what you wrote in sessions 6 and 8 about expectations and threats/promises.** Review the list of activities in question 4, and note whether the reason you can't get out of each activity is connected to a) someone's expectation of you; b) an expectation you have of yourself; c) a stated or implied threat of what will happen if you don't come through on this activity; or d) a stated or implied promise. Mark each item on your list with a, b, c, d, or no letter.

To regain control of your life and schedule, you will have to decide the degree to which you will be controlled by expectations, threats, and promises. In reality, you aren't locked into any of these activities. The question is whether you are willing to pay the price of not meeting your own or others' expectations of you.

6. When you think about not living up to your own or others' expectations in these areas, what goes through your mind?

7. If you were going to make the kingdom of God—or the love of God and neighbor—your top priority during the next month, how would your schedule be different?

"Jesus calls us to His rest, and meekness is His method. The meek man cares not at all who is greater than he, for he has long ago decided that the esteem of the world is not worth the effort. . . . The rest [Christ] offers is the rest of meekness, the blessed relief which comes when we accept ourselves for what we are and cease to pretend. It will take some courage at first, but the needed grace will come as we learn that we are sharing this new and easy yoke with the strong Son of God Himself."[1]

8. How would your schedule for the next six months be different?

9. Look back at your answers to questions 4-6 in session 3 and question 16 in session 6. Below are some suggestions for reducing your activity overload. (They are explained more fully in chapter 4 of *The Overload Syndrome.*) Check any that you want to put into practice. Then add any other ideas you have.

☐ **Lay your calendar before God.** Pray for guidance about priorities and areas for pruning. You might make this a daily rite first thing in the morning. God is able to get more eternally significant things done in twenty minutes than you can in twenty years on your own.

☐ **Practice saying "no" to good things**, even things you would enjoy if you had the time. Stand in front of a mirror and say *no* over and over until you get good at it. (If you know a two-year-old, take lessons).

☐ **Cross out items from your activity list** above (question 4) that you can reasonably cancel.

☐ **Commit to saying "no"** to any similar commitments people ask you to make for the next six months.

☐ **Plan empty space** into your calendar. If you have to look beyond six months from now to find uncommitted time, do it. Start setting aside blocks of time that you will refuse to schedule.

☐ **Resign from a long-term commitment** (other than your

marriage). Pray first, and see whether that committee or board is really one of God's priorities for you.

☐ **Make it a priority to eat at least four meals with your family each week.** If your kids are older than ten, enlist their help in planning these times for the next two months. Be flexible, but also be prepared to cancel some activities. If you can't cancel things, then start scheduling these meals together beginning next month or the month after, and agree together to refuse any activities that conflict with these family times.

☐ **Start scheduling four hours of rest** on Saturday or Sunday (or another day if your work schedule includes weekends). That is, four hours without errands, housework, yard work, or other tasks.

If you checked the above item, what will you have to give up in order to do this? Is it worth it?

☐ **Schedule a week away with no activities.** That is, instead of planning an action-filled vacation, plan one that is action-free. Go to a mountain cabin, for instance, with no electronics. Sleep when you get tired and wake when you've had enough. For the first few days, you may feel a withdrawal akin to panic. You may find out you've been keeping yourself busy to avoid what you might have to think and feel if you were alone with yourself.

"Let not the wise man boast of his wisdom,
   or the strong man boast of his strength
   or the rich man boast of his riches,
   but let him who boasts boast about this:
   that he understands and knows me,
   that I am the Lord, who exercises kindness,
   justice and righteousness on earth,
   for in these I delight."
(Jeremiah 9:23-24)

"You must ruthlessly eliminate hurry from your life."[2]

Hurry

10. **What threats or promises motivate you to hurry?** For example, some people think a busy person must be important. Some people are driven by fear of disappointing someone and so losing a job, a relationship, or someone's respect.

11. **Do you get enough sleep?** If not, what appear to be the activities that cut into your sleep time?

12. **Look back at your answers to questions 1 and 2 in session 4.** Below are some suggestions for reducing your hurry overload. (They are explained more fully in chapter 9 of *The Overload Syndrome.*) Check any that you want to put into practice. Then add any other ideas you have.

   □ **Practice breathing slowly.** Breathe in to a count of eight. Hold your breath while you count to eight. Then exhale very slowly to a count of eight. Practice this while you're driving, standing in line, or anywhere you have a few minutes.

   □ **Live for a week without wearing a watch.**

☐ **Stop using an alarm clock.** Your body was designed to wake up on its own when you've had enough sleep. If you're not getting enough sleep to wake up on time, try going to bed earlier. (You'll have to cut out some activities or work time.)

☐ If you're going to bed at what seems an appropriate hour but your body needs to sleep later, **rethink your schedule.** Is your commute time or distance unrealistic for your body's needs? Are you forcing your body to conform to the world's demands? Maybe it's the demands that need to change.

☐ **Value sleep.**

☐ **Buy a good mattress**—you will spend a third of your life there.

☐ **Set an earlier Estimated Time of Arrival** so that if something goes wrong, you don't have to rush. Don't feel it's inefficient if you arrive early. To set an earlier ETA, you may need to set an earlier Estimated Time of Departure. You may not be able to hurry through quite as many tasks before you leave.

☐ **Plan a day where you live with only the technology of 1930, 1900, or 1850.** Walk, read, talk, and sleep, but just accept that you can't get anything done that requires our modern, hurrying technologies. This experiment will show you how much of the pace of your life depends on these devices. Schedule this day on your calendar sometime in the next six months.

☐ **Make a list of activities** you do in a given month that serve productivity but not spirituality or relationships. Cross as many of these items off your schedule as you can.

How well did you sleep last night? What do you think would help?

☐ **Schedule time with family and friends each week** for the next two months. Put relationships ahead of productivity. On page 148 ("Actions Steps to Take This Week") write, "Schedule time with (list names)."

☐ **Schedule at least an hour a week to wait on God** in solitude. God won't be hurried and, in the long run, waiting on God is the most productive thing you can do. Wait on God to know His ways and His priorities for your life. Then you won't waste time doing things that aren't important.

☐ Other ideas:

Emotions

The five previous sections address areas in which you are probably experiencing overload and need to cut back. This final section addresses an area you are probably neglecting and need to build up. You'll need to cut back in the other areas to build up your emotional reserves. But while reading through the ideas above, you may have found that your emotional reserves are so low that you can hardly imagine making an effort in those areas. If so, you are like a surgical patient who is too weak to undergo an operation. You need to be strengthened with emotional nourishment before your life can handle the stress of the surgery you desperately need.

13. Many of the above ideas will help you rebuild emotional margin. However, here are some other ideas to start with. (They

are explained more fully in chapter 7 of *Margin*.) Check any that you want to put into practice. Then add any other ideas you have.

☐ **Love, affection, nurturing, intimacy, connectedness, empathy, community**—these are the nutrients that replenish emotional reserves. If you find yourself emotionally empty, go to a caring friend. Talk to someone who has the capacity to listen and respond with understanding. Make a regular habit of this. Clear space in your calendar for this priority.

I have found that, regarding emotional margin, there are three kinds of people: those who fill you, those who just sit there, and those who drain you. Unfortunately, the drainers outnumber the fillers about two to one (not a scientific number). And some of those drainers really deserve our attention—children, for instance. But if we already feel drained and have experienced too many draining relationships, we may have a habit of withdrawing for survival. Isolation, though, prevents us from reviving. The obvious answer is not to abandon people, but to learn how to make our relationships mutually nourishing. If you can't think of a friend who will listen, don't be afraid to talk to your pastor, your doctor, or a therapist.

☐ **Pet a surrogate.** Physical touch nourishes our souls. If you can't get a few hugs or handshakes a day, get a pet. Choose something furry that you can stroke. Pets bond, are extremely loyal, and show deep appreciation for your affection. All of these will build your emotional reserves.

☐ **Reconcile relationships.** Make a list of people whom you are finding it hard to forgive. Beg God for the grace to yield your right to get even. You don't have to like the person; just pray to let go of the desire to make him or her pay. Pray for a vision for what he or she could be if transformed into Christ's image. If appropriate, pray for a restored relationship. Likewise, make a list of people whom you have wronged. Confess your sin to God. If appropriate, take the first step toward making amends with the other person.

☐ **Serve others.** Some of us are already overcommitted in service, but for those of us who are caught up in our own agendas twenty-four hours a day, a regular habit of service would nourish our parched spirits. Start in simple ways: when you enter a toll highway, pay not only your toll but that of the person behind you. Hold doors open for people. Bring bagels for your administrative staff.

☐ **Rest.** If you have an office with a door, close the door for fifteen minutes in midafternoon each day, turn off the phone, sit comfortably, and close your eyes. If you can't relax in the office, take a half-hour walk. Or set Wednesday mornings as quiet days when you take no calls.

☐ **Envision a better future.** A vision for the future builds hope. Without hope, emotional life shrivels. "Hope deferred makes the heart sick," says Proverbs 13:12. Take a few minutes right now and describe what you believe in and want to work for that is higher than yourself.

☐ **Practice gratitude.** Right now, list ten things for which you are thankful.

☐ **Grant grace.** The next time someone does something that annoys you, purposely choose to treat that person better than he or she deserves. Cut the person some slack. Try this once a day and see what happens.

☐ Other ideas:

14. What thoughts and feelings are going through your mind after considering action steps in six large areas of your life? (For instance, does this feel like more tasks for an already overloaded schedule? More decisions for an already overburdened brain? Or does it feel like a relief? Are you fearful of what might happen if you made these changes?)

The LORD is close to the brokenhearted
    and saves those who are crushed in spirit.
    (Psalm 34:18)

If you're feeling overwhelmed by all the changes you think you should make in your life, start slowly. For instance, you might select just one action you want to take this week (and write it on page 148). You might choose just four things you want to take care of this month and four next month. In two months, you'll have taken action in eight areas! If this seems like too much, you can start smaller still. But remember, you are making these changes to *reduce* your sense of overload. The actions you are taking should clear time in your calendar, not add to it.

15. What are three action steps from this session that seem especially important for you? Be sure to record them on the "Action Steps" lists on pages 148-153 .

For Groups

Talk about how helpful (or unhelpful) it has been to consider all these action steps. What are you feeling about the process? (Overwhelmed? Relieved?) Some overloaded people may experience this list as another load of expectations, or they may feel frightened that their house of cards may tumble if they start tinkering with it. Do you need to take the process more slowly? Is there anything you can do to make sure it's an aid rather than a load?

Also, some people may find they can't make time for some of the actions in this session until they have dealt with issues addressed in session 12, especially work and money.

It will be important not to create a competitive environment in the group, in which people feel they have to keep up with each other in making radical changes. Strive for an atmosphere of encouragement (literally, "to give one another courage") rather than judgment. People who are used to competing and excelling can easily make simplicity another area in which to compete. People who take pride in giving advice may be tempted to fix each other's lives. A helpful group norm might be to give no advice unless a person requests it. Feedback from group members about strategies to reduce one's overload can be enormously valuable if it is given and received in an encouraging, redemptive spirit.

Share with one another your lists of action steps. Ask for support and help in carrying them out. You may want to do some things together. You may be able to help each other think through how to make an idea work in your unique situations. Look also at your lists of action steps you'd like to take but don't believe you can. What are the obstacles? Can the group suggest solutions?

Notes

1. A. W. Tozer, *The Pursuit of God* (Harrisburg, PA: Christian Publications, 1948), p. 112,116.
2. John Ortberg, *The Life You've Always Wanted: Spiritual Disciplines for Ordinary People* (Grand Rapids, MI: Zondervan, 1997), p. 81.

ACTION STEPS TO TAKE THIS WEEK

ACTION STEPS TO TAKE THIS MONTH

ACTION STEPS TO TAKE NEXT MONTH

ACTION STEPS TO TAKE CONSISTENTLY FOR THE NEXT SIX MONTHS

ACTION STEPS TO TAKE
SOMETIME IN THE NEXT SIX MONTHS

ACTION STEPS I'D TAKE IF I COULD

Taking Action II

In this session you will make an action plan for six more areas of your life: change, choice and decision, work, debt, possessions, and physical energy. Once again, the first five are areas in which you may be overloaded, while the sixth is one that will help you rebuild your strength. Your objectives in this session are:

- To find steps you can take that will create margin in your life
- To consider both the costs and benefits of taking these steps
- To evaluate this plan according to two criteria: Is it realistic? (That is, do the benefits outweigh the costs?) And, will it help me love better?

Below are ideas for action in the six areas listed above. As you read through them, have your calendar handy to schedule exactly when you are going to do the items you choose. Mark only items that you seriously intend to do in the next six months. Write them on one of the Action Steps pages (pages 148-153). If you find an idea that you wish you could do but can't for some reason, write it on the page, "Action Steps I'd Take If I Could."

As you go through this process, you will notice some connections. For example, the less time you have, the more you need to pay for services like fast food, gift-wrapping, and yard work. The more you need to pay for services, the more money you need. The more money you need, the more you have to work. And the more you work, the less time you have. Therefore, cutting back in one area requires (and enables) cutting back in other areas. If you want more time for people and yourself, you will need to work less and spend less. More for people means less for things. There's no way around it.

Before you begin this session, ask God for the wisdom to make good choices, the creativity to see how to increase your margin without sacrificing the things that are most important to you, and the peace to accept the limits in your life.

Change

Different personalities have different tolerances for change and routine. Some people are easily bored without variety. Others are easily overwhelmed by too much variety. Many people are somewhere in between. A hundred years ago, society was run by the traditionalists, and people who needed more variety were sometimes mistrusted. Today, our leaders in society tend to be those who love lots of change, so most of us need to work at creating consistency. Before you consider the suggestions in this section, assess your personality preferences: How much change do you need to thrive? How much consistency do you need to thrive? Also, assess the personalities of the people you live with. Do you live with anyone who needs more consistency than your lifestyle is providing? How can you structure your life together so that everyone's needs are considered?

1. Look back at your answers to questions 7-9 in session 3. Below are some suggestions for reducing your change overload. (They are explained more fully in chapter 5 of *The Overload Syndrome.*) Check any that you want to put into practice. Then add any other ideas you have.

    ☐ **See a counselor to take a life-change index.** It will tell you if your current overall rate of change puts you at risk for physical or emotional illness.

    ☐ **Put on hold any decision about a change of job** for six months.

    ☐ **Don't move** this year.

    ☐ **Don't build a house** this year.

    ☐ **Stick to one church** for the next year.

    ☐ **Decide to put down roots somewhere.** Invest in relationships there.

☐ **Don't overvalue newness.** When tempted to switch or buy, ask yourself, "Is new necessarily better?"

☐ **Resist upgrading for a year.**

☐ **Create as much routine in your spiritual practice as will help you.** That might be as little as setting the same time each day in the same spot for prayer. Or, it might mean adopting a pattern for Bible reading, prayer, and meditation that you will stick to for the next six months.

☐ **Develop a network of caring friends.** Find at least three people with whom you can share frustrations and good times. Invest time in these people.

☐ **List the names of at least three people** in whom you would like to invest time and energy for relationships:

☐ **Join a long-term small group.** Make it a priority.

☐ **Limit your time with negative people.**

☐ **Do something kind for someone else.**

☐ **Select a vacation spot you can go to every year,** rather than going someplace new each time. Select a restful place: a cabin by a lake or a condo by the ocean. Vacations do not have to be exhausting exercises in accumulating new experiences.

☐ **Choose to take control of your response** to stressful circumstances. Research shows that events affect us less negatively if we feel we have some control. You may not be able to control the situation, but you can control your choice to rise above it. If you are facing a stressful situation that you can't control, make your response to it a topic of prayer.

☐ **When you start worrying, catch yourself.** Remind yourself that worry doesn't accomplish anything. Tell God what you're worried about.

☐ **Look for something to laugh about every day.** Laughter lowers blood pressure and pulse, and it seems to improve immune functioning.

☐ **When you make a mistake, laugh at yourself** rather than berating yourself.

☐ **Play relaxing, uplifting music.**

☐ **Meditate on the consistency of God.** God will never change His high value of you, will never abandon you, and will never change the rules without telling you. Circumstances change, but God's trustworthy character never changes.

☐ Other ideas:

Choice and Decision

You have plenty of time to decide on this action plan.

2. Look back at your answers to questions 10-13 in session 3. Below are some suggestions for reducing your choice and decision overload. (They are explained more fully in chapter 6 of *The Overload Syndrome.*) Check any that you want to put into practice. Then add any other ideas you have.

   ☐ **Simplify your wardrobe.** For example, select one or two basic colors that you like (black, brown, beige, navy, khaki), and begin building your wardrobe around those colors. Schedule two hours some Saturday to weed out everything from your closet that you haven't worn in the past two years. Give it to a thrift shop. Unless you really enjoy variety in wardrobe, try to pare back to a minimum wardrobe. How many pairs of pants/skirts/shirts do you really need? On pages 149 and 150 "Action Steps to Take This Month" and " . . . Next Month" write three things you'll do to simplify your wardrobe.

   ☐ **Simplify meal choices.** For instance, you might eat the same breakfast every day except for Saturday, when you have a special Saturday breakfast. Rotate the same dozen menus for family dinner.

   ☐ **Make a list of decisions you are currently facing,** from trivial to substantial. For each major decision, write down what information you need to make it wisely. If it's helpful to do so, schedule when you're going to gather this information. Also, schedule time for solitude and waiting on God. (Did you do that in session 11?) If you take that time alone, you can expect God to speak or leave the decision to you.

   ☐ **Pray for wisdom.** Make your decision list a topic of prayer each day. But don't obsess about it.

   ☐ When you do decide, even on insufficient information, **stick to your decision.** Maintain an open mind and be open to new information, especially about spiritually significant things. But don't keep revisiting decisions about spiritually insignificant things like insurance. For a full year, ignore all telephone or mail solicitations about long-distance phone service, insurance, newspapers, charities, and so on.

□ **Decide on the basis of long-term consequences,** not immediate gratification.

□ **Mistrust advertisements.**

□ **Ignore marketing gimmicks.**

□ **Fast from decisions for a week or longer.** Deliberately postpone all decisions for that period. Use it as a time to wait on God and recharge your decision batteries.

□ **Value traditions.** Establish some traditions for holidays and celebrations.

□ **Own your decisions.** You are not trapped by your boss, your family, or your debts. You live in a world of your own choosing. If you feel trapped, write a list of things in your life that you chose. (You chose this job. Do you want to unchoose it?) You don't have the power to change everything in your life, but you can identify the choices you already made and the ones you can still make.

□ **Choose your attitude.** Even people who live in concentration camps have the freedom to choose to be generous, loving people.

□ **Daily rechoose the things of God.**

□ Other ideas:

Work

Look back at your answers to questions 10-12 in session 4. Also, think about what you've written about threats, promises, and expectations related to work.

3. If you are overworking, which of the following factors are motivating you to do so?

☐ I need to pay off debts.

☐ I am trying to afford a lifestyle that emphasizes possessions and entertainment.

☐ I am recently divorced and starting over.

☐ I am a single parent with children to care for.

☐ I can't support my children on a forty-hour workweek.

☐ I have major medical expenses.

☐ Wages in my job category are not keeping up with inflation.

☐ My company has downsized, so those of us who are left have to work overtime to keep our jobs.

☐ I'm afraid I'll lose my job if I ask to cut my hours.

☐ I look to my work for my sense of self-worth, identity, purpose, direction, and/or community.

☐ The important people in my life value me for my work or my income, not for my capacity for relationship.

☐ I value my achievements at work more than I value the people closest to me.

☐ I value possessions more than I value the people closest to me.

When Daniel's three friends stood up to their boss, he ordered them to be burned alive. They replied: "O Nebuchadnezzar, we do not need to defend ourselves before you in this matter. If we are thrown into the blazing furnace, the God we serve is able to save us from it, and he will rescue us from your hand, O king. But even if he does not, we want you to know, O king, that we will not serve your gods or worship the image of gold you have set up." (Daniel 3:16-18)

☐ I feel more at home when I'm at work than when I'm at home.

☐ Other factors:

4. Put a star by those factors motivating you to overwork that are things you can do something about. What can you do?

5. Below are some suggestions for reducing your work overload. (They are explained more fully in chapter 13 of *The Overload Syndrome.*) Check any that you want to put into practice. Then add any other ideas you have.

☐ For the next couple of months, **focus your prayer and Bible reading** around the issue of where your identity comes from. Start reading through the book of Ephesians, for example, with this question in mind. When you're finished with Ephesians, start through Matthew. Ask God to build in you a sense of identity, significance, and value based in Him, not in work.

☐ **Face your fear of job loss or career stagnation** if you ask to cut back your hours. For the next month, focus your prayers on those fears. Ask God what you should do.

☐ **Identify people in your life who value you** for who you are rather than what you do for a living. Make a priority of spending time with those people.

☐ **Be cautious of promotions.**

☐ **Investigate flextime**, job-sharing, and telecommuting.

☐ **Cut down your commute time.** You might go in early (and leave early) or go in late (and leave late). You might telecommute two days a week or even full time. You might move closer to work or find a job closer to home.

☐ **Insist that your employer allow you a private life**— time during which you cannot be reached for work by pager or cell phone.

☐ **Tell your employer the truth:** You cannot do more and more with less and less.

☐ **Be prepared for resistance from superiors when you set boundaries.** Consult the book of Daniel, chapters 3 and 6. Daniel and his friends were bureaucrats who drew the line.

> I pray that the eyes of your heart may be enlightened in order that you may know the hope to which he has called you, the riches of his glorious inheritance in the saints, and his incomparably great power for us who believe.
> (Ephesians 1:18-19)

☐ **Develop interests outside work.** If you are not already over-committed with activities, take up a hobby, give yourself in service to the less fortunate, or befriend an international student.

☐ **Make your family a priority.**

☐ If work is more pleasant for you than home because home relationships are in disorder, **face the disorder and commit your time and energy** over the next year to doing what you can to remedy it. What is the first step you can take in this direction?

☐ **Assign high value to the domestic work of motherhood.** If you're not the mom in your home, value the person who is. If you are the mom, value yourself.

"Measure wealth not by the things you have, but by the things you have that you would not take money for."[1]

☐ If your work conditions are overly stressful and the hours unreasonably long, **consider a job change.** But think and pray first. The grass is not necessarily greener on the other side of the fence. And don't leave your job until you have another lined up; the stress of unemployment and rising debt may be worse than the stress of overwork.

☐ **Bring the kingdom of God to bear in your work.** Whenever you encounter another human being, decide to relate out of love, not just out of commerce.

☐ Other ideas:

Debt

A man is a slave to whatever has mastered him.
(2 Peter 2:19)

6. Why do you spend? Check any that apply:

   ☐ I spend because I enjoy the experience of buying.

   ☐ I spend when I'm depressed.

   ☐ I spend when I'm bored.

   ☐ I try to buy my way into others' hearts.

   ☐ I buy because of peer pressure.

   ☐ Spending gives me a high feeling.

   ☐ Spending makes me feel I'm successful, not poor.

   ☐ I spend because . . .

7. By now you have been keeping track of your expenses for almost three months. Gather your expense sheets, and add up the totals in each column for Month 1 and Month 2. This task may seem tedious, but if you have trouble spending less than you earn, doing this will give you priceless information. It will tell you where your money is going. (If the very idea of adding up all these numbers puts you in a cold sweat, do you dare ask a friend or someone in your group to do it for you? You could even recruit one of your children—permit an extra hour of video-game time for every hour spent adding numbers.)

   On page 166, record your total expenses in each of the nine areas. Then add up the nine figures for Month 1 to get your total expenses for the month. Do the same for Month 2.

TOTAL EXPENSES

MONTH	Groceries	Clothing	Housing	Utilities	Entertain-ment	Health Care	Grooming/Exercise	Auto	Other	TOTAL

8. What do you learn about yourself and your priorities from your expenses? Do any of the figures surprise you?

9. Overspending and debt are major causes of overwork. Look back at your answers to questions 4-7 in session 4. If either overspending or debt is a factor in your overload, below are some suggestions for reducing your expenses. (They are explained more fully in chapter 7 of *The Overload Syndrome*.) Check any that you want to put into practice. Then add any other ideas you have.

☐ **Commit to a budget.** Tracking your expenses for three months is the first step toward creating a realistic budget. You are already well on your way toward doing this. Your next step might be to buy a book that will guide you through the process of budgeting. Larry Burkett and Ron Blue both have excellent ones.

☐ **Say no to new purchases** (other than bare necessities) for six months.

☐ **Don't go to a mall for six months.**

☐ **Throw away catalogs** as soon as you receive them.

☐ **Don't buy anything on credit** for six months.

☐ **Cut up your credit cards** and throw them away.

□ **Don't buy anything when you first see it.** Think and pray about it for a day or a week. See if it's a need or just a desire.

□ When thinking about a new purchase, review your answers to question 6. **Why are you spending?**

□ **Consider moving** to a smaller home.

□ **Keep appliances** until they die in your arms.

□ **Stop venerating automobiles.**

□ **Eat out less.**

□ **Set an expense ceiling** for Christmas and birthdays.

□ **Enjoy free activities.**

□ **Institute this four-step process** for paying off debt:

- List all debts in order, from the smallest to the largest.
- Pay at least the minimum payment on each debt each month.
- Double payments on the debt at the top of the list whenever possible.
- As each debt is paid off, apply that payment plus the minimum payment toward the next debt.

□ Find a person or group who will keep you honest. **Discuss your expenditures** with them at least once a week.

□ Other ideas:

> "Eighty-six percent of those Americans who have voluntarily cut back on their consumption say they are happier as a result."[2]

Possessions

Just as debt is a major cause of work overload, so the drive to own more things is a major cause of debt. Getting out from under the burden of things may be the key to freeing up your time, physical energy, and emotional energy for people. Look back at your answers in session 6. Think about your expectations about possessions.

10. Below are some suggestions for reducing your possession overload. (They are explained more fully in chapter 12 of *The Overload Syndrome.*) Check any that you want to put into practice. Then add any other ideas you have.

   ☐ **See owning as a liability** rather than an asset. Every possession requires time and energy to care for it.

   ☐ **Make a list before you shop,** and stick to it.

   ☐ **Make a clutter date with a friend.** Spend the afternoon clearing out one of your closets. Spend another afternoon the following week clearing out one of your friend's closets.

   ☐ For your next birthday party, **ask your guests to come to your home and take something away.**

   ☐ **Commit some time each week to comparing yourself to the poor, the ill**—anyone who has less than you. Put yourself in their shoes. Do something actively compassionate. This will help counteract the tendency to compare yourself to people on television, in advertisements, and elsewhere who have more material things than you.

   ☐ **Make friends** with some people who will support you in a simpler lifestyle. Peer reinforcement can work for you rather than against you if you spend time with the right people.

   ☐ **Share things with friends.** Maybe each household doesn't need its own chain saw, Rototiller, canoe, tents. . . . List some items you can share rather than buy:

☐ **Ignore the lifestyles of the rich and famous.** Don't buy magazines that tell you what they wore to the Academy Awards or how they've decorated their houses.

☐ **Go through the list of expectations** you made in session 6. Revise downward your expectations regarding possessions. Write down what you will be content with:

☐ If you struggle with revising your expectations downward, **think about why:** Are you afraid of what people will think? Will you feel like a failure? Does success = possessions or does success = love?

☐ For what kinds of possessions do you have a special weakness? (For example, consider clothes, electronics, tools, cars, home furnishings, jewelry.) **List the things you gravitate toward** in catalogs, the mall, anywhere you shop:

□ Other ideas for dealing with your possessions:

Physical Health

Just as you need margin in finances, time, and emotional energy, so you need margin in your physical life. You may need to cut back in other areas (such as activity, work, and possessions) to rebuild in this area.

11. Below are some suggestions for adding margin to your physical life. (They are explained more fully in chapter 8 of *Margin.*) Check any that you want to put into practice. Then add any other ideas you have.

   □ **Get enough sleep.** We mentioned sleep in session 11, but it's important and neglected enough to revisit. It's important not to oversleep (that can make you feel more tired), but more and more people today suffer from sleep deprivation. How much sleep does your body actually need each night? Not "How much were you able to survive on when you were twenty?" but "How much do you need on a regular basis now?"

   □ **Develop healthy sleep patterns.** Many people don't sleep well simply because they practice poor sleep habits. A healthy pattern is to retire at a similar time each evening and arise at a similar time each morning. Sleep in a quiet room with a good mattress. Don't engage in disturbing conversations or watch action-packed television before bedtime. Instead, begin relaxing about an hour before retiring. Don't have a big meal within two hours of retiring.

■ **If sleep is delayed by racing thoughts**, keep a notebook or even a small tape recorder beside the bed. If insomnia strikes, don't panic. A few nights of sleeplessness will only make things worse, and panic is a sure way to drive away sleep. Instead, get out of bed, sit in a comfortable chair, read, write a letter, have a light snack, take a walk, play relaxing music, or watch low-key television. But don't worry. Consider turning the night into a conversation with God. Pray. Listen. Meditate. Read the Bible. Begin a spiritual journal. And don't forget to thank God for the special opportunity of this time together. When you begin to feel tired, go to bed with gratitude for the double blessing of fellowship and sleep.

Which of these ideas seem relevant to you? How would your life have to change for you to get enough sleep?

■ **Develop an exercise program**. Good conditioning will make you more energetic and efficient for all other endeavors. Note that being "on the go" all day is not the same as getting exercise. Just because you come home tired every day doesn't mean you are building endurance and strengthening your heart. In fact, thirty to forty-five minutes of *sustained* exercise three times a week will actually help your blood vessels deliver blood to your body and make you feel less tired at the end of a busy day. This kind of exercise is a primary key to physical margin.

Exercise in the evening after an exhausting day is difficult for many people. Discouraged, they give up. On the other hand, morning exercise energizes people for the day. If this is true for you, choose morning exercise. If possible, go to work later and work later to make time for exercise in the morning. Other people, however, find that evening exercise after a stressful day drains the stress from their bodies and gives them renewed energy for the evening. Much of our exhaustion from office work is emotional rather than physical.

If exercising is hard for you, identify the reasons (I don't enjoy it. I don't have time. . . .). List the reasons here.

Then address the reasons. For instance, find a place where you would enjoy walking. Walk with a friend if you can. Cut something else from your schedule to find three hours a week for exercise. Or use an exercise bike and catch up on your reading while you cycle.

If you checked this item, describe your plan for building an exercise program. If all you can think of are reasons why you can't exercise, then on page 149 ("Action Steps to Take This Month") write, "Find a creative solution to my exercise dilemma."

☐ **Eat less fat.** We all know we should eat less fat (not more than 30 percent of our daily calories), but we eat it anyway. There are three main reasons: It tastes good, it is our habit, and we can afford to. In rebuttal, there are other things that taste good, we can change our bad habits, and we can't afford not to. Good nutrition begins not in the kitchen but in the grocery store. If it isn't good for you, don't buy it. If you can't help yourself, send someone else.

☐ **Avoid grabbing fast food on the run.** Many of us eat more fat than we should simply because we don't have time to buy, make, and eat a healthier meal. While healthy fast food is increasingly available (and is a better choice than burgers or tacos), we can save both money and health by taking ten minutes in the evening to make tomorrow's lunch. We'll need a little time margin to do this, but the physical payoff can be significant.

☐ **Avoid processed foods with high sugar content.** These include sugared cereals, breakfast pastries, candy, small cakes, chips, gum, juice, and soft drinks. Check package labels: if "sugar," "high fructose corn syrup," or "dextrose" appears as one of the first three ingredients, don't buy the item. And don't give in to children's requests to buy these items either. Ninety-five percent of the food ads on Saturday morning television are for high-sugar products, so it's no surprise children ask for these products. Just as we need to learn to say "no" to overload in work and activities, we need to learn to say "no" to advertising's influence on our kids. They may complain now, but the seeds of diabetes, heart disease, and obesity are sown in childhood.

☐ **Replace processed snacks with fruit.** We often bypass fruit, thinking it is too expensive. However, cookies, chips, and candy are usually even more expensive.

☐ **Drink a lot of water:** six to eight glasses a day.

☐ Other ideas:

Review

12. Review the plans you made in this session. Add your plans to the "Action Steps" lists on pages 148-153. What will it cost you to cut back in these ways?

13. What will be the benefits of cutting back?

14. What are you feeling right now?

15. Do you believe the steps you've decided to take will significantly affect your load six months from now? If not, describe your misgivings. They might point to a deep issue that is more important than all the minutia. Or they might simply reflect your emotional exhaustion. It's hard to be optimistic when you're drained!

16. Look at page 153 ("Actions Steps I'd Take If I Could"). If your other lists already seem long, set these items aside for now. Mark your calendar to take another look at them in six months. If you've scheduled half a day to be alone with yourself every six months, that would be a good time to review these steps that you've set aside. On the other hand, if you have a long list of steps you'd like to take and not many steps you feel able to take, spend a few minutes identifying the barriers that are preventing you from doing what you need to do. Describe those barriers.

17. You've completed this workbook! Do something good for yourself: enjoy a walk, take a nap, play some music, call a friend.

For Groups

Share your lists of action steps. Focus especially on items concerning work, money, and possessions. For most people those are the most challenging. You may have several action steps you'd like to take but don't believe you can. Some members of the group may be feeling paralyzed at the thought of creating a budget or even facing the math involved in calculating their expenses. You have been together for three months or more—can you trust each other enough to be honest about the things that seem impossible? Can you trust each other enough to ask for help with budgeting and cutting back? Chances are that everyone in the group needs some kind of help, whether practical (like working with numbers) or emotional (like support in having a tough conversation with a boss).

Save some time to bring your group to closure. Give each person a chance to say what he or she has gained from the group. In an extended prayer time, each person can thank God for one thing about the group and ask God for one thing for the other members of the group. It would be ideal to bring food to your final meeting so that you can celebrate what you have accomplished together. One question to focus this closure discussion might be the following:

- Picture yourself driving away from this meeting and seeing the other group members in your rearview mirror. What will you wish you had said to the people here?

You have a choice at this point. You can choose to end the group. But you could probably use some mutual support in your plans to gain margin in your lives. Consider meeting weekly, biweekly, or even monthly to report progress and get help addressing challenges. Some questions you could discuss in ongoing meetings include:

- What have you done since our last meeting to build margin into your life?
- What challenges are you encountering in your efforts to reduce your overload?
- What can the group do to help or support you?
- How can the group pray for you?

Notes

1. Russ Crosson, "Your Finances in a Changing World," Focus on the Family 1997 Physicians Conference, November 1997.
2. John deGraff, producer, "Affluenza," Public Television Special, first aired September 1997.

AUTHORS

Richard A. Swenson, M.D., is director of the Future Health Study Center and fellow at the Paul Tournier Institute. He received his bachelor of science degree in physics Phi Beta Kappa from Denison University and his doctorate from the University of Illinois School of Medicine.

Following five years of private practice, Dr. Swenson taught at the University of Wisconsin Medical School for fifteen years. His current focus is "cultural medicine," researching the relationship between faith, health, culture, and the future.

Dr. Swenson is the author of *Margin: Restoring Emotional, Physical, Financial, and Time Reserves to Overloaded Lives;* and *The Overload Syndrome: Learning to Live Within Your Limits.* He is a highly requested speaker on the themes of margin, stress, overload, complexity, and social change to a wide variety of career, professional, and management groups; most major church denominations; Congress; and the Pentagon.

Dr. Swenson and his wife, Linda, live in Menomonie, Wisconsin, with their two sons, Adam and Matthew.

Karen Lee-Thorp is a Senior Editor for NavPress, responsible for study guides and small group resources. She was editor for the LifeChange Bible study series and is author of many study guides. She has been published in *Christianity Today, Discipleship Journal, The Mars Hill Review,* and *Clarity.* Her books include *Why Beauty Matters, The Story of Stories, A Compact Guide to the Christian Life,* and *How to Ask Great Questions.* She holds a B.A. in history from Yale University. Karen lives in Pasadena, California.